PARADOX
AND THE
FAMILY SYSTEM

Camillo Loriedo, M.D.

AND

Gaspare Vella, M.D.

TRANSLATED BY

Maryanne Olsen, M.A., Ed.S.

BRUNNER/MAZEL, *Publishers* • NEW YORK

Library of Congress Cataloging-in-Publication Data
Loriedo, Camillo.
    [Paradosso e il sistema familiare. English]
    Paradox and the family system / Camillo Loriedo and Gaspare Vella;
translated by Maryanne Olsen.
        p.   cm.
    Translation of: Paradosso e il sistema familiare.
    Includes bibliographical references and index.
    ISBN 0-87630-635-0
    1. Family psychotherapy. 2. Paradoxical psychotherapy.
I. Vella, Gaspare.   II. Title.
RC488.5.L6613   1991
616.89′156—dc20   91-29684
                                                            CIP

Published by
BRUNNER/MAZEL, INC.
19 Union Square West
New York, New York 10003

MANUFACTURED IN THE UNITED STATES OF AMERICA
10 9 8 7 6 5 4 3 2 1

CONTENTS

FOREWORD

The steady growth of family therapy is evidenced not only by a many-fold increase in practitioners, but also by a many-fold increase in theories. In its own right it has become a territory for explanations, understandings, and explications of all that makes therapy useful.

Dr. Camillo Loriedo and Professor Gaspare Vella present a classic European scholar's approach to the subject of paradox, and to the whole territory of family therapy. Beginning with a veritable firestorm of logic, they describe the classic evolution of paradox with all its profound implications for the development of mathematical theory, the Theory of Logical Types, and the use of paradox in thinking. All of this, of course, precedes by many, many years, the application of paradox in psychotherapy. The orientation with their intellectual study of thinking and its application to psychotherapy practice proves its validity as well when applied to the field of research in psychotherapy.

The careful and repeated distinction between the use of paradox as a technical "trick" and the truthful utilization of the paradoxical process by serious and caring psychotherapists is "the difference that makes the difference" when working with the more difficult families that are now getting the courage to ask for help.

The presentation of paradox within a framework requiring the therapist being free to involve himself with the family, and then learn how to back away at the appropriate moment in therapy, is a beautiful example of the importance of honesty and authenticity in the therapist who uses paradoxical techniques.

The description of paradox as "a systematic ambiguity capable of producing undecidability by means of an infinite reflexive oscillation among different levels of complexity" presents the reader with a clear understanding of paradox and what this means in its application to the psychotherapeutic process.

Quoting Picasso that, "Art is a lie that makes us realize the truth" is only one of many delicious and thought provoking quotes that make us see clearly through the chaos of family therapy as a profession. To understand how simplification and complexity always coexist, and to hear through the fact that even irrational messages must include dignity, make it easier to know what the authors mean when they say that "complexity is essentially unpredictability." Moreover, the use of paradox is a means for therapists to become active participants in their own growth, and to avoid the burnout that can result from their "adopting" patients who then become, through their own sense of failure, bloodsucking components in that failure.

Enjoying such sayings as "crazy is freedom and freedom is crazy" makes me chuckle with a kind of delightful afterglow. Continued reading reveals what is really meant by an understanding of thinking, and an even deeper understanding of therapy itself. We learn that the success and failure of the paradox is not in its pattern of operation but in the therapist, himself.

The most enlightening experience for me in reading this book was an understanding that the assumption of illegitimate totality can be considered identical with the paradox. In a strange way, that rigidity which we find in a family belief system that is frozen can be used not only to understand the absurdity of the patient's symptoms, but as a way to further understand the pattern that makes paradox so useful. Of course, as the authors explain, all therapeutic paradox is really counterparadox, bringing us to a whole new level of understanding what the authors obviously already know, and explain so well.

The whole assumption that "man's pursuit of absolute truth is the child of his own desperation," is an example of complex European thinking at its best. This profound reasoning is then supported by extensive references and fascinating case material, illustrating not only how the therapy was successful, but including, as well, detailed definitions and categorizations of various kinds of counterparadox and techniques for their utilization. I find myself wondering, "Are these authors even tempting us to think that what's happening here could produce an illegitimate totalizing of the life of a psychotherapist? Could this lead to a new methodology for expanding his own work in a way he had not thought possible before?"

The memories of my many years of knowing and admiring the work of Camillo Loriedo and Gaspare Vella have added personal joy to revelling in this book. Reading it has certainly been an exciting experience for me. I expect it will be for you, too.

CARL A. WHITAKER

INTRODUCTION

The term *paradox* comes from the ancient Greek and indicates a condition that is seemingly contradictory, not congruent with accepted opinion, and opposed to common sense. This meaning determines its role in dilemmas and creativity and places paradox in a central position at the intersection of logic, philosophy, and the psychological sciences.

Within the psychological sciences, the study of paradox began with considerable delay, and only recently the pioneering work of Gregory Bateson and colleagues demonstrated its importance in human mental health and for the communication theory of schizophrenia. This delay explains why we currently have very little knowledge of how paradox influences human reasoning and of the possible applications of the concept.

The aim of this book is not only to stimulate interest in the psychological and interactive aspects of paradox, but also to clarify the therapist's role in the use of paradox by exploring more fully the definitions, applications, and implications of paradoxical therapy within the family system. The ten chapters contained in this volume constitute a comprehensive education on the subject, beginning with the evolution of paradox and ending with illustrative case examples.

The first step towards meeting the goals of the book has been our own study of disciplines more familiar with the intricacies of paradox. This has been the most difficult part in writing the volume, as it took a great deal of patience and sacrifice to think about our usual work with patients and families in a different way—to think in terms of the complex game of Logical Types Theory and the solution of the Barber paradox. We spent years reading books not usually found on a psychotherapist's bookshelves and discussing logical paradox with those so involved.

It was particularly difficult to translate for ourselves and for readers not possessing a sophisticated philosophical background the language of philosophy and logic in order to explain family interactions and therapeutic interventions. We hope readers will find this translation clear enough, and we also hope we didn't trivialize these confusing concepts.

Our choice was to present a theoretical frame of reference, highlighted by clinical examples. In our opinion, a better understanding of pathogenic and therapeutic paradox will greatly improve the quality of the therapist's work. We believe that this book will provide a valuable perspective on a subtle—but extremely powerful —side of reality, emphasizing that psychotherapy must be more than "technique" if it is to be effective.

The first chapter on the history of paradox presents a brief account of the evolution of paradox. The evidence shows that the development of paradox depends on the growth of knowledge: paradoxes of today can be solved tomorrow, but new paradoxes may arise. However, it does not seem that the progress of knowledge will cause paradoxes to disappear from life.

Since pathogenic paradoxes are able to suspend time in a given relationship, they appear to be more stable and redundant over time than the logical ones. By contrast, therapeutic paradoxes should evolve through time in accordance with the therapist's knowledge and the family's changes. The history of paradox also demonstrates that to solve logical paradoxes, attention, curiosity, and a sense of humor are necessary. The family therapist who uses therapeutic paradox should possess the same qualities.

In Chapter 2, we explore the importance of Russell and Whitehead's *Principia Mathematica* and Godel's *Theorum* in regard to the current notions about paradox: The Assumption of Illegitimate Totality is a convincing explanation of how paradox develops in logic. We also consider this explanation as a key to understanding the Pragmatic Paradox and its pathogenic and therapeutic effects on human systems of interaction.

The so-called *new logic* appears to be parallel to the development of new epistemologies in human sciences, particularly General Systems Theory and Cybernetics, where the idea of *complexity* emerges and imposes new ways of conceptualizing human problems and their solutions. The following three chapters (3, 4, and 5) are dedicated to the description of the origin of paradox in human relationships in terms of complexity; paradox is defined as "an *illegitimate totality* that produces a violation of a complex hierarchy." Thus a model for understanding the onset and maintenance of severe pathologies is traced and the consequent therapeutic strategy is outlined.

In Chapters 3 and 4 the ingredients of paradox and their connections are examined so that the complex understructure can be revealed. Common ingredients come together so that two different alternatives become possible: a passage to higher levels of knowledge (*recursive chain*) or the activation of an infinite vicious cycle (*reflexive chain*), which does not allow access to new learning.

Illegitimate totality as the core nucleus of the reflexive chain (Chapter 5) has its roots in some inherent aspects of human relationships, particularly in family systems relationships (Chapter 6). Fundamental to the development of paradox in a family system is the contribution of both the individual members, with their own paradoxical beliefs, and the family system itself, with its inner convergent or divergent totalities.

In Chapter 7 we go over the differences and similarities between pathogenic and therapeutic paradox, an area neglected in the current literature. We maintain that differences should be clear in the therapist's mind in order to enact effective therapy. A number of these differences demonstrate that therapeutic paradox really isn't a true paradox, and in our opinion, the term *counterparadox* is more appropriate to describe the use of paradox as a therapeutic intervention.

A classification of therapeutic interventions (Chapter 8) is of great value in the process of selecting the proper intervention for every single case: Counterparadoxical therapy should be very carefully suited to the individual patient or family, in contrast to pathogenic paradox, which keeps repeating itself regardless of the situation and context in which it takes place.

Guidelines to construct a counterparadox and the general philosophy for its use are presented in Chapter 9. Emphasis is placed upon the facts that counterparadox isn't simply a technique and that it is not based on the therapist's skill only. Counterparadoxical therapy involves a certain general attitude and the stance of the therapist in front of individuals, families, and their dysfunctional patterns: Respect and confirmation of both persons and patterns are primary factors for inducing change through paradox.

Clinical cases are presented in greater detail in Chapter 10 in order to show the many forms that counterparadox can assume in therapeutic practice. Counterindications to using paradox in therapy, such as dangerous behaviors, are also described to help the therapist avoid the common misuses of therapeutic paradox as well as to prevent the therapist from getting into a situation of illegitimate totality.

Finally, we want to underline the role played by the therapist in the use of paradox. Too many clinicians consider paradox to be an effective trick and they behave consequently: They don't believe in what they prescribe, they just believe in its effect. In our experience, we find that if the therapist doesn't believe in the counterparadox given to the family, the family isn't able to trust therapy and, as a result, will not be able to change.

Paradoxical therapy requires a profound change in the therapist's mentality, a change that requires a special kind of training to see the less obvious side of reality and to understand its complexity. In our opinion, dramatic modifications of family behavior can take place only if this change in the therapist happens: Studying the nature of paradox and learning how to apply it in therapy is one possible way for the therapist to reach this goal.

CHAPTER 1

✦✦✦✦✦✦✦✦✦✦✦✦✦✦✦✦✦

THE ORIGINS AND DEVELOPMENT OF PARADOX

PARADOX IN THE FAMILY: A LIVING DOLL

Clara feels everything around her is menacing and threatening her life. For more than three months, she has been afraid to go to sleep, fearful that someone will enter her bedroom and kill her; she eats less and less because she suspects that all her food and beverages have either been poisoned or contaminated. She insists on preparing her own food and checks all beverages provided by her parents. Sometimes she smells everything first; then every bottle or glass is carefully inspected as she suspiciously checks their contents for strange objects which may have been placed within.

With each passing day, Clara considers not just food and drink dangerous but nearly everything else. She suspects that even the air is contaminated and threatening her life. She vigorously attempts to gain control over her entire environment.

1

Her parents try to reassure her that no one wants to kill her. They even eat and drink in front of her, attempting to prove that what they are giving her is safe. Despite their constant reassurances, they cannot change her mind.

Just as Clara becomes more and more convinced that danger is in *everything*, her parents insist that *nothing* is dangerous to her. Instead, they maintain that in order to survive she has to eat and drink.

Here, we are faced with two conflicting convictions. Clara is sure that she will be destroyed by exactly the same things that the parents think she needs to survive; the parents are afraid that what Clara thinks she needs to do to survive will surely destroy her. Because of their own unsatisfying childhoods, they believe they have an obligation to keep her happy and safe.

Clara's mother, Irma, was born "by accident," as she put it, to a couple who was close to divorce. Shortly after her birth, Irma's father and mother did divorce. The mother, thereafter, seemed to be resentful toward Irma, as though her birth precipitated her husband's asking for a divorce. As Irma related the story to Clara, her father resented having this added responsibility at a time when the marriage was already in serious difficulty. Whether Irma was accurate or not in evaluating her mother's rejection of her, her perception of her childhood experience was that she was not cared for and felt that she had been deprived of both material and emotional needs.

Later on, Irma met and married Antonio, a much younger man, because, she stated, he needed "someone who liked him and could help him." Antonio was described by her as "poor and ugly" and she believed that if it were not for her, he would never have married. Antonio accepted Irma's nurturing attitude as a "piece of sunshine" in his life of loneliness and despair: he had been orphaned at the age of 5, when both his parents died tragically in a fire. Antonio was rescued from the fire by a neighbor who heard his cries, but she was unable to save his parents.

This same neighbor then asked for and obtained an unofficial adoption agreement from Antonio's relatives. She raised him until her own death three years before Antonio's marriage to Irma. Antonio describes this event as a "horrible period of emptiness. . . ." He explicitly states that Irma was, for him, a substitute for the parental figures he had lost in both his distant and recent past.

When Clara was born, both Antonio and Irma decided that she would never experience the deprivations that they had suffered. They considered Clara to be fragile from the beginning and gave her their undivided attention to meet any need. They made financial sacrifices so that the best physical care and schools, and the most expensive foods, could be provided for Clara. They devoted all their efforts to making her happy and healthy. To ensure this, they decided not to have any more children so that she could continue to benefit from all of their physical and financial resources.

When Clara had her first dating experience her parents encouraged and supported her. They seemed to be under the impression that if someone else cared for her, they could finally achieve their ultimate goal: the guarantee of a normal and satisfying life for Clara. They had not experienced life satisfaction and they secretly feared it would not be attainable by their daughter. After some months, when Clara ended the relationship with her boyfriend, they considered this their failure; their loss of her future security and happiness.

The thought of their daughter remaining alone and unloved threatened and terrified them. They both reported the day Clara ended her relationship as the "worst experience" of their lives, even though many other events in either of their lives could doubtless be considered more tragic.

The parents questioned Clara's reason for the breakup of her relationship and attempted to find ways to mediate the problem. When they failed, they compensated for their daughter's "loss" with more and more devotion and care. Their constant attention compounded Clara's problems; it inhibited her moving toward the outside world, which seemed less and less desirable and rewarding compared to what she received at home. Before long, the parents recognized they were caught in an impossible dilemma. The more love, affection, and care they gave her, the more attached to them she became.

The dilemma became apparent a few days prior to Clara's first refusal to eat and drink any food and beverages without inspecting them, perceiving as dangerous everything her parents gave her or did for her. She became suspicious and defensive; her fears escalated, and their relationship deteriorated. Months later in a family therapy session, they described this period as full of uncertainty and with a sense of feeling "stuck" for the whole family. The underlying beliefs and assumptions that created the family's problems, making it "a living hell," were still intact and are revealed through a transcription of the dialogue in the first session:

Father: It is like all that we thought was most important for our daughter has suddenly become like poison for her.

Mother: She refuses *everything she needs.* . . .

Clara: I don't need what *you* think I need; I need to control what I eat. You can eat what you want and I will eat what I want. I don't want to die from what you give me.

Mother: We only want to give you *what you really need.*

Clara: It is crazy. . . .

Father: I have the feeling that the more we try to help her, the worse the situation becomes. I honestly don't know what to do and actually feel impotent.

Clara: I'll tell you what to do. Leave me in peace, *give me my independence*, rent me an apartment in which I can feel safer than I can here. Stop cooking for me, stop squeezing the oranges for the juice you want me to drink, and stop preparing my coffee.

Father: Well, I don't think we have enough money to rent an apartment for you, but if the doctor says it is what we should do, we will do *everything he says.*

Mother: But if she lives alone, she probably won't eat at all.

Father: Yes, but if the doctor suggests we do it, I think we should do it for her.

Mother: This is an impossible situation; if we help her she hates us and becomes more suspicious, and if we don't help her, she could die from starvation.

Father: She *should become more independent*, to see for herself that she has to eat only for her own sake. She *should be using her own will.*

Mother: We dedicated so much time to her and made all sorts of sacrifices . . . sometimes I think of Clara as a beautiful doll. We created a very beautiful doll and we put all our energy and our hopes into her: the best clothes, the best shoes, we groomed her perfectly but, now, finally we have to admit she is only a doll; we have to admit that we gave her everything except the one thing that is truly necessary, and would have made our work worthwhile. *We are unable to give her independence from us.* Despite our efforts, she remains a beautiful, perfect, doll . . . but just a doll.

Many readers will be able to recognize in the above transcription some transactions that have been described as paradoxes by Gregory Bateson and his associates (1956) in their work at Palo Alto. The concept of double bind and paradox was very important to them, not only as a key to understanding schizophrenia in context, but also as a possible explanation of many family entanglements.

Paradox has also been employed therapeutically to intervene in and dissolve these family entanglements. The concept of paradox, both the pathogenic and the therapeutic, has an obscure nature, and this book is dedicated to bridging the logical concept with its application to clinical work with families. We propose that a general knowledge of paradox and its nature is important to recognizing and understanding the intricacies and complexities resulting from its emergence in human interaction, due to its inherent ambiguity and subsequent undecidability, as occurs in many family dilemmas.

To clearly demonstrate the therapeutic utility of paradox in present-day clinical application, the differences between pathogenic and therapeutic paradoxes will be presented, including the distinction between paradox and similar concepts with which it is often confused. When therapeutic paradox is practiced properly, it can be adapted to the family's own individual situation. At this point, we will highlight some cues in Clara's family that will be explored more thoroughly throughout the text.

The tendency to think and to speak in terms of *totalities* is evidenced by the description previously given by the parents: *everything* is dangerous or *everything* is safe. This either/or condition is found to be a central theme in the paradoxes found in dysfunctional families. As we will see, terms such as "all," "every," "always," and "never" are a common denominator of pathogenic paradoxical statements.

Another aspect that Clara's family exhibits very clearly is the paradox of individuation, which is beautifully described by the metaphor of the doll Clara's mother used at the end of the dialogue. When she stated, "We are unable to give her independence," she expressed the undecidable paradoxical dilemma of parents who want to *give* individuation to their children. The harder they try, the less the children will receive anything but further dependency.

We will see, in subsequent chapters, how individuation cannot be prescribed and how the tendency to prescribe it isn't the consequence of a "bad" or "crazy" family system. Rather, it derives from experiences in which individuation is perceived both by the parents and the child as an *absolutely necessary* goal to achieve. The histories of Clara's parents could explain their desperate efforts to raise her as they did.

On the other hand, Clara's participation in the process

is indicated by her request, "Give me independence," which is paradoxical as well since independence cannot be requested as an absolute; it requires taking responsibility for self.

The family's descriptions of their assumption that one could be either loved or rejected, either married or alone are only two examples that demonstrated their belief that reality is an either/or process. These and other aspects of a dysfunctional system recognizable in Clara's family will be reviewed as we continue. Connections will be made with logical aspects of paradox in light of the Theory of Complexity which is, in our opinion, the central idea with which to gain access to an understanding of functional and dysfunctional systems of human interaction.

Paradox is a complex phenomenon; its definition is not an easy task. Watzlawick, Beavin, and Jackson (1967) describe it as "a contradiction that follows correct deduction from consistent premises" (p. 188). According to this definition, paradox seems to be an unexplainable contradiction that creates difficulties in understanding. We will, for the moment, accept this definition. Later, in Chapter 5, we will present a new definition, which we consider even more descriptive of paradox, in terms of a violation of the principles of complexity.

The remainder of this chapter is dedicated to tracing the development of paradox from its earliest known origins and to describing and clarifying its nature.

Since introduced by Zeno in the sixth century B.C., paradox has always held a certain fascination for man. During the late nineteenth century, this fascination led to paradox being the catalyst and the basis for many arguments in logic and mathematics. More recently, it has received considerable attention in the fields of psychology and psychotherapy, where paradox has developed into a powerful instrument for changing human behavior. In following this development, we pave the way to a broader understanding of the applications of paradox to human interactive processes and to present-day psychotherapeutic techniques. The complex implications of paradox appear to have pragmatic effects on the emergence of some types of pathology and, when utilized as a therapeutic instrument, on some forms of psychotherapy.

A BRIEF HISTORY OF PARADOX

Historical evidence shows that the first to consider the phenomenon of paradox, around 500 B.C., was Zeno of Elea, son of Teleutagora and student of Parmenides. Zeno was not considered an ordinary man; he was often referred to as a noble, albeit rebellious, spirit. Zeno strongly defended the teachings of Parmenides, whose philosophical and political beliefs led to his capture and death after an unsuccessful attempt to depose the tyrant, Nearco.

According to Aristotle (Rose, 1886), Zeno was the originator of paradox and of dialectics: "His method was to reduce his opponent's hypotheses to absurdity by deducing from them contradictory consequences" (Fragment 65). Zeno's speculations on paradox were undoubtedly the primary reason for his recognition among the presocratic philosophers and for his importance in the history of philosophy and logic and, later, in mathematics.

Zeno's paradoxes have also provided an abundance of thought to mathematics. Paradox, especially today, is an important subject for study and discussion in many fields. Recently it has received considerable attention in the fields of psychology and human behavior. The complex implications of paradox appear to have pragmatic effects on the emergence of some types of pathology and, when utilized as a therapeutic instrument, on some forms of psychotherapy.

To understand paradox more clearly and to allow a greater understanding of its pragmatic aspects, we will describe briefly some of its developmental changes and transitions that have ocurred over time. While we cannot offer an exposition here that would be regarded as thorough or extensive, we can begin with Zeno's most noted paradoxes and, thereafter, deliberately limit our study to the logical aspects of paradox that may have direct or indirect relevance to human behavior.

Zeno proposed his paradoxes (among the best known is that of Achilles and the tortoise) to uphold the theories of his teacher, Parmenides. Parmenides stated that true being is immutable and immobile and that the plurality of things and motion does not exist. This theory provoked, understandably, much criticism from the philosophers of that period. Some went to the point of rejecting the Parmenidian Proposition on its unrealistic premise. They argued that motion and movement do exist and that they have demonstrative behaviors, such as rising and setting out for a walk.

Zeno responded to their criticisms with the following

absurd argument: A tortoise placed at any distance from the swift-footed Achilles will never be overtaken by him. In fact, Achilles must first reach the starting point of the tortoise, from which the tortoise will already have advanced to a new point. This, of course, would continue for each new starting point. Consequently, the tortoise will always maintain his advantage, even if minimal.

Zeno further elaborated on the use of paradox to demonstrate that movement does not exist with another of his best-known paradoxes, that of the arrow in motion. Referring to an arrow shot from a bow, Zeno affirmed that every object that occupies an expanse of space equal to itself can either be at rest or in motion. However, at the interior of the expanse of space equal to itself (the space required by the size of the arrow), nothing can move and, therefore, is at rest. As the arrow continues in its flight, it will continue to occupy, in every single moment, an expanse of space equal to itself. It follows, then, that it can only remain at rest. Thus, if the arrow is motionless in every second of the time in which the action is occurring, it will be motionless for the entire time. Since it was presupposed that the arrow would be in motion, it would have to be at rest and in motion simultaneously.

Zeno's logical and unassailable arguments led, ultimately, to absurd paradoxical conclusions. It must be emphasized that Zeno did not wish to support the validity of his conclusions, only their absurdity. Nevertheless, because we draw correct deductions, logically consequent to the reality of the premise, these conclusions tend to demonstrate the falsity of the same premise and, therefore, the truth of the proposition so dear to the Eleatic school, which considered motion as simply appearance, and being as one and immutable.*

Aside from his political positions, Zeno was not very popular among his contemporaries. His work was scorned as Sophism. However, after more than two thousand years, the sophisms of Zeno have reappeared as being valid. They undoubtedly supplied the starting point for Karl Weierstrass's (1815–1897) development of a new mathematics and the elaboration on his *Theory of Limits*.

Weierstrass rigorously excluded the infinitesimal and asserted that it is possible to demonstrate that at every moment of its journey an arrow is really in a quiet state and that the world in which we live is considered, at every single moment, actually immutable. Perhaps the point at which Zeno made a mistake was in deducing, if indeed he did, that if there is no fundamental change in every single moment, then the world would remain in the same state even in its own subsequent moments. His deduction did not result as an absolute from the previous premise.

Paradox and dialectics, as introduced by Zeno, initiated over time a radical change in the history of logic. This change forced revisions of some principles that had previously been accepted as absolute truths. Paradox has permitted us, for example, to grasp the limitation of the Aristotelian "Principle of Contradiction" which states, in

---

*Those who are aware of the psychotherapeutic approach of Carl A. Whitaker will recognize many analogies to Zeno's reasoning. Whitaker never emphasizes directly to the family the emotional and behavioral incongruencies that take place within it. Usually he prefers to develop and exaggerate behaviors to their extreme consequences, to the point at which their absurdity becomes apparent.

essence: "It is impossible that contradictory propositions are contemporaneously true" (Aristotle, *Metaphysics*, Book XI, 1966).

The recognized existence of paradox has induced a revision of a great number of absolute convictions or, we may say, has opened the way to the idea of "complexity." In a later work, Aristotle affirmed, "With regard to an affirmation, and an opposite negation, it is not always necessary that one of them is true and the other false" (Book V, 1946).

Since Zeno, then, the human mind has continually been tested with new formulations of paradoxes, followed by attempts at more or less effective solutions. If readers are interested in investigating more paradoxical enigmas that logic has proposed over time, they may easily locate them in the bibliography of this book. Instead, we present, though in a necessarily synthesized form, the passages that led us to consider paradox a mode of relationships in human interaction: a modality that can have a determined influence on the health of the individual and of the social groups in which he takes part.

Following this line of reasoning, we move from Zeno's purely logical and therefore abstract paradoxes, without attention to the immediate impact on behavior, to the paradox of the liar. This is a paradox; yet it may be more accurately defined as an "antinomy" or a paradoxical definition which includes a self-definition by the person who presents the paradox. It carries, therefore, not only messages of content but also of nonnegligible messages about the relationship. This paradox does not have a purely speculative value; it identifies a true paradoxical relationship.

THE FIRST PRAGMATIC PARADOX

The "Liar Paradox" was erroneously attributed to Epimenides, a man noted for his wisdom, who lived in Greece in the sixth century B.C. At the time of Epimenides, however, the term "paradox" was not yet in use; it was recognized as such only around 330 B.C. Diogenes Laertius's (1950–1951) accounts are more reliable. He attributes the discourse of the liar to Ebulides of Megara who lived in that period.

Many diverse versions of this paradox have been compiled, and it is practically impossible to state which is the original. Nevertheless, they all lead to the same essential statement: "If I say I lie, and I lie, I then speak the truth." It is not difficult with this affirmation to clearly identify the consequent vicious circle. In fact, whoever says it speaks the truth only if he lies, and he lies only when he speaks the truth. This vicious circle also implies pragmatic consequences. A speaker or a listener would be unable to determine the extent of truth and falsehood of the statement. All significant interactions and relationship possibilities become suspended and undecidable.

The enigma of the liar, even with the diverse ways it has been described, leads us to the first dramatic results of paradox on human behavior for which we have proof. The logician Philetas of Cos (340–285 B.C.), in an attempt to resolve the enigma, neglected his own health to the point of death, as shown in his epitaph:

> Traveller, I am Philetas; the argument called The Liar and deep cogitations by night, brought me to my death. (Bochenski, 1970, p. 131)

Before discussing the ways in which paradoxes exercise their effects on human behavior, we consider it necessary to examine briefly the evolution of the concept of paradox in modern logic. This examination seeks to illuminate, in the next chapter, some of the background research necessary to understand the underpinnings of the concept of paradox, and why Gregory Bateson (1956), with his collaborators, chose Whitehead and Russell's "Theory of Logical Types" from *Principia Mathematica* (1910) as support for his hypothesis on the origin of schizophrenia. In addition, Bateson (1972b) has affirmed:

> Insofar as behavioral scientists still ignore the problems of the *Principia Mathematica*, they can claim approximately sixty years of obsolescence. (p. 279)

Despite the determinant role played by the Principia in the development of the Double Bind Theory and, therefore, in the subsequent evolution of the systemic perspective, the Principia was, and remains today, one of the lesser known and even less investigated aspects of these disciplines. For that reason we will dwell upon some of its major concepts in an attempt to integrate them, as much as possible, into the framework of which the paradox of classes, and the Theory of Logical Types designed to solve it, have been developed.

CHAPTER 2

❖❖❖❖❖❖❖❖❖❖❖❖❖❖❖❖❖❖❖❖❖❖

FROM THE PRINCIPIA TO GODEL

Paradox in the New Logic

"More than once in history the discovery of a paradox has been the occasion for a major reconstruction at the foundations of thought."
—W.V. Quine, *The Ways of Paradox and Other Essays*
(1966, p. 3)

THE ANTECEDENTS OF THE PRINCIPIA

The ideas expressed by Whitehead and Russell in the *Principia Mathematica* (1910) were so completely innovative in character that they "shook the foundations of mathematics," as Gottlob Frege, much to his dislike, was forced to acknowledge.

Frege, an academician and researcher bound to strict scientific rigor and methodology had been, moreover, the first to conceive a mathematical logic. When he became aware of these ideas, he was also forced to reconsider his entire monumental work, *Grundgesetze der*

Arithmetik (1893–1903). In an appendix to the conclusion of this work, Frege admitted with regret:

> It is very difficult for a scientist to encounter anything more undesirable, than to see the foundation of his work collapse at the actual moment in which he has concluded it. I was placed in this position by a letter of Bertrand Russell. (Quine, 1962, p. 13)

Nevertheless, the work of Frege, and above all his *Begriffsschrift* (1879), contains a series of fundamental perceptions proposed with a semantic and descriptive accuracy that has been compared to the Aristotelian Method.

Specific to our present interest in Frege's work, it is important to remember that he was the first to make a distinction between language and metalanguage. Much of what was discovered through his observations were included by Russell and Whitehead in the *Principia Mathematica*.

Russell and Whitehead also built upon George Boole's *The Mathematical Analysis of Logic* (1847), another antecedent of the *Principia Mathematica*. Boole, the originator of symbolic logic, utilized algebra and its formulas to explain the paradoxes of logic. Thus, for the first time, a metalanguage (different from the language proper of the same discipline) was used to describe a discipline and to demonstrate its coherence; hence, it has been termed "metalogic." Whitehead and Russell accepted Boole's premises, but they inverted the principle and resorted to logic in order to explain mathematics. In this way, they formalized what Hilbert (1928) defined as "metamathematics": a language designed "to establish mathematics on a more reliable basis" (p. 66).

After Boole, then, it became universally recognized that rules of logic are found at a different (meta)logical level with respect to simple mathematical formulas, and to the logical processes, or to the communicative actions that these govern.

From Frege to the Principia the idea of levels becomes crucial in the field of logic. The concept of levels developed by Russell and Whitehead constitutes the basis for the Theory of Complexity, the theory that is currently considered a quantum leap in understanding the organization of systems and, particularly, of the family system.

Metalanguage and the Family Therapist

Like language and metalanguage in logic, human communication is now described in terms of a common language and of another more complex language that comments on the former and has the power to change its meaning. Whatever message we convey with words can be simultaneously or, shortly thereafter, changed by our metalanguage. Family therapists have learned to be aware of the importance of metalanguage. They know that in a family there are always two different forms (or levels) of conversation going on at the same moment. For this reason a family therapist may speak of very trivial subjects, knowing that the metalanguage will be nevertheless very meaningful. Hence, given the higher complexity of metalanguage, even a very rich and seemingly insightful conversation in a family has little value compared to what could become intelligible to an observer "listening" to the metacomments of the family members. According to this principle, the literal content of a "family secret" loses its relevance when compared to the more complex patterns that accompany the process of revealing or concealing the same secret. What is important in a family interview is not to obtain "the truth" but, rather, to look at how *the different truths of the family are presented and perceived.*

We owe to Gregory Bateson (1972b) the application of metacommunication, a term coined by Whorf (1956), to interactive contexts. The profound intuition of Bateson was evidenced by his outlining the role played by the relationship between the different communication levels to human dysfunctional behaviors. He further pointed out the relationship between language and metalanguage, considered significantly relevant to most common errors in logic.

THE PRINCIPIA MATHEMATICA

Along with the concept of levels, another seminal idea that brought Russell to the Principia was a quest for a noninferential language, the "thread of Arianne." Leibniz thought such a language among scholars would eliminate any discussions that were not resolvable with a calculation. Russell used the concept of "propositional function" to describe his explanation of paradox by means of a noninterpretational metalanguage. A propositional function differs from customary mathematical functions in that the values of the function are expressed by propositions. Since these propositions can be represented by mathematical variables, it is possible to subject them to calculation.

A propositional function is characterized by a variable (an *x*, for example) that can assume a number of different values. Therefore, the propositional function is, by definition, ambiguous. In practice then, any proposition can be converted into at least one possible value of a propositional function. This is, of course, very useful in logic where there is a continuous need to use propositions with possible different meanings. It is also applicable to human communication in which there are a series of propositions (interactive exchanges and messages) that are often endowed with ambiguity. The ambiguity of the propositional function was used intentionally by Russell and Whitehead to explain the "Vicious Circle" paradox on the basis of the Theory of Logical Types.

As we have seen, a propositional function is characterized by a variable *x*. All the values that can be assigned to *x*, in order for the propositional function to have meaning (range of significance), constitute a logical type.

- The *first logical type* (the lowest) is represented by a single term or *individual*. According to Whitehead and Russell (1910), an *individual* "is something which exists on its own account" (p. 162).
- The *second type* is constituted of all the individuals that satisfy some propositional function; these together form a *class*. It is possible, as well, to replace the concept of class with that of *relationships*, a term more commonly referred to in our field. "All terms or individuals that have with other terms any relation *r* form a class" (Russell, 1903).

• The *third type* is a class formed by members that are classes and, therefore, is a *class of classes*. If a class is analogous to the concept of relationship, a class of classes is a relationship of relationships and, therefore, a *system*.

Russell justifies this subdivision of all objects into types as necessary to avoid the fallacy of the vicious circle, or *illegitimate totality*. These fallacies are produced because of the *systematic ambiguity* of some terms, among which Russell placed the concepts of truth, falsehood, function, class, relationship, name, definition, and so on. Thus, Russell made a distinction between two types of ambiguity: simple ambiguity and systematic ambiguity.

Simple ambiguity happens when a term or a proposition has many possible meanings but they are all contained in the same logical type. A *systematic ambiguity* is a special type of ambiguity in which some of the possible meanings belong to different logical types.

A simple ambiguity doesn't transgress the principles of complexity and cannot, by itself, create a paradox. A systematic ambiguity is necessary in order to determine the assumption of illegitimate totality that constitutes a paradox. Similarly, in logic, in human systems in general, and, particularly, in families, ambiguity per se does not create the greatest problem. What does create confusion and dysfunctional interaction is the type of ambiguity that contains an illegitimate totality—a systematic ambiguity.

When a husband tells his wife a number of seemingly unconvincing stories about why he must go away for a work weekend, his wife may look for some cues in his ambiguous behavior to determine whether he is lying or telling the truth. Some uncertainty may exist in her mind, which could make her uncomfortable with his explanation, but that in itself could be resolved.

But let us suppose that at some point the husband has said to his wife, "I can't be trusted." The ambiguity then becomes systematic because the phrase contains a statement that contains the phrase, making it undecidable. If the husband is not trustworthy, then the wife shouldn't trust what he says and, so, he will be trustworthy. But if he *is* trustworthy, then she should trust his statement that he is not trustworthy, and so on.

Systematic ambiguity constitutes the prerequisite for the violation of logical types that determine the paradox. Actually, *a type cannot contain an individual which, by its inherent systematic ambiguity, also contains the superior logical type.*

A propositional function should not have within itself a proposition that contains it; neither should a class (paradox of classes) contain in itself a class of classes. As Whitehead and Russell (1910) assert, "Any expression containing an apparent variable must not be in the range of that variable, i.e., must belong to a different type" (p. 161). Therefore, a class cannot be an element of itself; a class of classes cannot be one of the classes that is its element; a name of a thing is not the named thing itself. As Bateson (1972a) suggests, "It would be like eating the menu card instead of the dinner" (p. 280).

Propositions of the type expressed by means of a function have the same ambiguous character that constitutes the rule in the statements made by the members of families with psychotic interaction patterns. For example, in the course of a family therapy session, the statement "Someone must speak"* by the identified patient implies that he or she expects that another family member will begin talking. The ambiguity of the statement consists in not indicating who must speak: the mother, the father, the brother or sister, or the identified patient.

We have limited ourselves in this example to the verbal ambiguity of the phrase for purposes of simplification. If we examine the analogical components in this type of human communication, we discover many more forms of ambiguity. For example, the identified patient's tone of voice may indicate that everything the family said up to the present was not "completely honest"; therefore, the family should "stop beating around the bush." The statement could also be interpreted as a threat or a warning to some or all family members, or as an attempt to fill a pause that is perceived to be anxiety provoking in those present. In the following chapters, we will see the importance communicative ambiguity can assume in a family system.

Whitehead and Russell (1910), in order to explain the logical paradox, introduced a series of concepts: the hierarchy of levels and complexity, systematic ambiguity, vicious circle, and illegitimate totality. All are of great interest for understanding human interaction according to the systemic perspective.

Bateson utilized the Theory of Types as the foundation for his studies on learning and for the Double Bind Theory. Undoubtedly, he was aware of the im-

---

*One statement of this type could be expressed in the form of a propositional function: "x must speak"; "x" represents the variable, and the ambiguity of the proposition depends on the nondefinition of the variable.

portance of the Principia and probably understood its applicability to human systems more than the authors themselves. Bateson (1979) himself states:

> Whether Whitehead and Russell had any idea when they were working on the Principia that the matter of their interest was vital to the life of human beings and other organisms, I do not know. Whitehead certainly knew that human beings could be amused, and humor generated, by kidding around with the types. But I doubt whether he ever made the step from enjoying this game to seeing that the game was nontrivial and would cast light on the whole of biology.
> (p. 116)

Notwithstanding some criticism directed mainly at form, the essence of the *Principia Mathematica* was exceptionally well received by scholars of logic and of paradox. In particular, it was generally accepted and subsequently developed the necessity, demonstrated by Russell, to set limits within any conceptual system to avoid falling into the trap of the illegitimate totality. From this perspective, we can understand Hilbert's (1928) choice to limit one's demonstrations to processes that are "finitistic" only and, therefore, are based on a well-defined (not infinite as was previously thought) number of structural properties.

We may understand also, from this same perspective, the so-called "limitative theorems": Church's Theorem of Undecidability, Turing's Halting Theory, Tarski's Truth Theorem, and, above all, Godel's Incompleteness Theorem.

GODEL'S THEOREM

When Kurt Godel described his Incompleteness Theorem in 1931, he was just 25 years old and his work, for some time, was scarcely noticed. Then, in 1952, after he was conferred an honorary degree from Harvard University, his work became recognized as one of the most important advances of logic in modern times.

One of Godel's major accomplishments is his elaboration of a purely *numeric metalanguage*. Starting from the conceptual system of the *Principia Mathematica*, Godel expanded it and translated each single formula into as many numerical expressions. While Russell preferred to use logic to discuss mathematics, Godel uses mathematics to discuss mathematics. Moreover, Godel's numeric metalanguage is not only designated to represent single expressions, but with appropriate extensions it may also represent the relationships between the expressions. In this way, Godel demonstrates the disposition of a keyboard which allows the production of both individual sounds and a complex symphony.

To fully appreciate Godel's demonstrations, one would need to understand the diverse theorems and 46 preliminary definitions. Given this complexity, all of which is not directly relevant to our work, we will touch only briefly upon some of the Incompleteness Theorem's more significant aspects. An excellent presentation, accurate, and at the same time relatively simple, the Incompleteness Theorem can be found in the Nagel and Newman (1958) essay, *Godel's Proofs*.

Godel examined formal systems used up until that time by means of his numeric metalanguage in order to test the coherence of mathematics and, in particular, the coherence of the *Principia Mathematica*. In the extensive and complex "gear system" of the Principia, Godel inserted a tiny grain of sand that revealed the capacity to block the entire mechanism.

The grain was represented by the arithmetic *Formula G*, translatable in current language: "Formula G is not provable." As in the "liar paradox," we find ourselves faced with a formula that affirms its own undemonstrability (the pragmatic value of this affirmation will be examined in Chapter 5).

Godel succeeded in demonstrating that Formula G, even though unprovable (by definition), is true if the mathematics is coherent. The result is the surprising conclusion that not only the Principia, but any other descriptive formal system of mathematics, even more complex ones, contains within itself unprovable propositions and, consequently, is incomplete.

By demonstrating the presence of undemonstrable propositions (in coherent, formal systems), Godel's Theorem reveals a paradoxical nature. As Watzlawick (1981) emphasized, the arguments of Godel demonstrate that "undecidability can be decided" (p. 329). As we shall see later on, the undecidable not only can, but must necessarily be decided.

Some theorists have drawn the conclusion that the theorem could determine the collapse of the conceptual framework of exact science, but this is largely an unjustifiable conclusion. Actually, Godel (1931) limited himself to demonstrating the untenable position of systems which are considered "sufficient to decide all mathematical problems that can be expressed formally" (p. 173).

To synthesize, Godel criticizes omnicomprehensive systems and shows their vulnerability through a paradox that proves their incompleteness. From this point of view, even the Principia demonstrates its weak point: in attempting to eliminate *all* forms of paradox, even Whitehead and Russell have fallen into the trap of illegitimate totalities.

The error that Godel uncovered in the Principia is the authors' presumption that it is possible to eliminate *every* form of paradox from human reasoning. In spite of this error, the importance of the Principia remains in the construction of the Theory of Logical Types and, particularly, in having grasped the essence of paradox. When Godel proved the incompleteness of Whitehead and Russell's system, he confirmed the validity of the *illegitimate totality principle*, which still remains a cornerstone in logic and, as we shall see, in pragmatics.

THE NEW LOGIC*

The system of the Principia, criticized by some and exalted by others, has produced a strong impetus for research, leading to what more recently has been defined as "Modern Logic." This new logic is characterized by at least three aspects:

1. The presence of a *metalanguage* that becomes distinct from so-called *object language*. This distinction be-

---

*Turn to the Logical Terms Glossary on p. 209 for definitions of words and phrases used throughout this section.

tween the object under observation that one studies,
and the discussion made about the same object, is
necessary (as the Principia has taught) to avoid in-
curring a paradox that could render the statement
undecidable.

2. The use of an *artificial language* with a formal structure, purposely elaborated to simplify the discussion,
avoids the semantic pitfalls of conventional language.
As an example, the concept of disjunction, expressed
in the natural language as "or," is usually represented
in formal languages by at least three different terms
with corresponding meanings that remain ambiguous in everyday language.

3. The *objectivity* of the logical procedures obviate any
form of subjective evaluation and, above all, any in-
terpretive attitude.

The aforementioned characteristics of the new logic
can, in large part, be attributed to the revolutionary
changes brought about by the Principia. These new ideas
make it possible for us to be aware of the profound
influence Russell and Whitehead's work has had on the
study of human behavior in general and on the systems
perspective in particular.

In fact, the systems perspective:

• places notable emphasis on the study of the human
metalanguages, as play, art, metacommunication, and
so on, in order to understand the interactive behavior and explores the languages suitable to describe
them.

• led to the development of *artificial languages* that are
more accurate; the most significant is Von Berta-

lanffy's (1968) General Systems Theory language.*
• allows the development of new, more objective, and
  noninterpretative methods of inquiry on patterns of
  human interaction.

This evolution of the systems perspective indicates the
profound effect that the Principia has had both on the
pragmatic and on the epistemological aspects of the approach.

Following the ideas presented in the Principia, logic
became, for the first time, *applied logic.* In reality, logic
has always been considered a discipline, important above
all for its applications but, in fact, the influence of logic
on a pragmatic world was only an indirect one. The new
logic, instead, is directly applicable to many fields with
remarkable results, and the most notable among these
is in the field of cybernetics and human systems. It is
for this reason and for implications of the distorted logic
of some human beings on their behavior and relationships that we consider the knowledge of pathogenic paradox so important to those who treat either individuals
or families.

---

*Often we forget that General Systems Theory, in the intention of its
author, must be a metalanguage and must be able to render mutually com-
prehensible but different scientific epistemologies.

CHAPTER 3

◈◈◈◈◈◈◈◈◈◈◈◈◈◈◈◈◈◈◈◈◈

THE RECURSIVE CHAIN

"An opposite can agree with its opposite, but even more beautiful is the harmony of discordances."
—Heraclitus, Fragment 8

An interesting analogy between human relationships and the mathematical concept of "function" was proposed by Watzlawick, Beavin, and Jackson (1967). Function consists of the relationship between two or more variables. The analogy is not only formal but extends itself to the level of the epistemological implications of the two terms. The transition *from* the idea of a finite number or finite quantity *to* one of function—that is, one variable that only has value when considered in relation to other variables—has marked a turning point in the field of mathematical thought. The impact of this significantly innovative concept can be considered in many aspects similar to that which occurred in the behavioral sciences with the introduction of the concept of *systems*, as compared to the more traditional concept of the *individual*. Whitehead and Russell (1910), commenting on the concept of function, say:

The question as to the nature of a function is
by no means an easy one. It would seem, however, that the essential characteristic of a function is its *ambiguity*. (p. 39)

AMBIGUITY IN INTERPERSONAL RELATIONSHIPS

Ambiguity constitutes still another important point at
which the concept of function and that of relationship
meet, and it assumes particular value in the field of
interpersonal relationships. Interpersonal relationships
are inherently ambiguous, and even more so in the family where they are subjected to critical transformations
throughout the different stages of the family life cycle.
These transformations can induce a number of changes
in both meaning and in the interactive patterns of the
relationship. Therefore, no one can ever be considered
as an absolute for every situation that occurs as the family progresses in its development. To do so runs the risk
of creating a severe dysfunction in the interactive processes of the family, such as that which occurred in the
following case:

> Carla, the anorectic 18-year-old in the Bocci
> family, complains of the difficult relationship
> she has with her father: a relationship which
> she describes as "icy." She claims she can no
> longer stand his inflexibility and its crippling
> effect on her.
> Carla explains that it has been this way for

as long as she can remember. She asserts she has tried everything she can think of to bring them closer, but nothing ever changes. No matter how hard she tries, her father continues to be as rigid and authoritarian as ever.

According to Carla, she has never had room to grow or to get close to her parents as an adult. Their view of the parent-child relationship is a hierarchical one and doesn't allow for the possibility of change to occur, even though she is no longer a child.

Her father interrupts her complaints, asking her to be more specific. Carla begs him to be willing to bend a little—to be more flexible. She asks him to recognize that she is no longer a child and that she now should have more freedom which would lead to more independence. Carla claims that the only way her parents communicate with her at all is by giving her rules; they never just share thoughts and feelings about the events in their lives.

At that, her mother commented: "We never thought that was the way to raise a child. In our family everything has always been somewhat formal. I don't know if I believe that it is even possible for relationships between parents and children to change as the children get older. Maybe we need to try seeing things differently if it will help."

Ambiguity in relationships occurs mainly through analogic communication; this form of communication has a major influence when problems arise during the developmental life cycle of any given relationship. A word, a gesture, as well as a verbal and/or nonverbal metacommunication can simultaneously take on different meanings in analogic communication.

From this perspective, in some behavior and interactive patterns, ambiguity can be considered not only inevitable but, to some degree, even desirable. In regard to this, Whitehead and Russell (1910) state:

> By employing typically ambiguous words and symbols, we are able to make a chain of reasoning applicable to any one of an infinite number of different cases, which would not be possible if we were to forego the use of typically ambiguous words and symbols. (p. 65)

Ambiguity is, therefore, necessary when one wants to describe or comprehend all possible terms, which can run the gamut of an infinite range of values. Similarly, ambiguity is inevitable in human relationships where a wide range of indefinable and indefinite possible behaviors in one individual encounters at least as wide a range of possible behaviors in another individual.

The importance of ambiguity and of ill-defined messages is such that, without them, our language would be deprived of its imagination, its symbolism, its humor, and its artistic expressions: that is, all of its more human aspects. It would then be reduced to no more than a mechanistic, Morse-like code.

CONTRADICTION IN INTERPERSONAL RELATIONSHIPS

Ambiguity is the logical premise and the efficient cause of an important pragmatic effect: *the contradiction*. When a relationship between two persons reaches a certain level of importance, every ambiguous sign becomes interpreted as a contradiction between two or more diametrically opposed alternatives. Consequently, identification of contradictory alternatives stirs up confusion, doubt, and suspicion. At some point, the need arises to attribute a meaning that is not ambiguous or contradictory.

For example, if a husband returns home late at night and tells his wife that he is late because he was detained with a client, any nervousness that transpires during his attempt to defend himself becomes an ambiguous message which his wife may interpret as an expression of two possible alternatives:

1. He is nervous because he feels guilty for not having informed her he would be late.
2. He is nervous because he has lied.

Since contradiction under any circumstance is poorly tolerated in and by most human beings, a search for *one* simple truth is initiated. The wife will look, therefore, for other indications in order to resolve any doubt and to verify which of the two hypotheses is more tenable.

In this case, as with ambiguity, a simple contradiction is not enough to create a paradox. There are not even enough elements present to determine a pathological relationship. Mehrabian (1981) warns:

> We must be cautious in identifying inconsistent messages with psychological disturbance. With our implicit social rules and prohibitions about the expressions of feelings (particularly negative ones), people frequently must use inconsistent messages. They may also use these to achieve effective communication, or even to be funny. (p. 55)

In our tendency to search for an unequivocal meaning in the messages we receive, we often overlook an important reality in our own way of communicating: the act of communicating carries with it the existence of many possible and simultaneous meanings.

In order to clearly illustrate this, Ashby (1956/1971) gives an explicit example: Let us suppose that the wife of a prisoner wants to tell her husband that an accomplice has been arrested, and they have worked out a plan beforehand to transmit this information through her by asking him if he wants a cup of coffee. Ashby makes the hypothesis that the guard, suspicious of the attempt to transmit a message, wants to block it:

> The guard will, more or less, reason as follows: The wife could have made an agreement with her husband to give him the news by whether or not she puts sugar in the coffee and to exclude this possibility, it is sufficient that he, himself, puts in more than enough sugar, and let

them know it is already in. If instead, the agreement was to transmit the message by putting or not putting a teaspoon together with the cup, he can take it, saying that the rules prohibit giving a teaspoon. If she had, instead, agreed to communicate by sending tea instead of coffee, it could be prevented by stating as fact that the administration allows only coffee at that time of day. These thoughts of the guard could go on and on, but the importance is that before every possibility, he seeks intuitively to prevent the communication by reducing it to only one: coffee, sweet, without a teaspoon, only coffee, and only in this way. The sooner the possibilities are reduced to only one, the sooner the communication is blocked, and the drink is deprived of its power to transmit information. (p. 156)

Ashby emphasizes strongly that the transmission and the retention of information cannot be connected to one single element, but depend necessarily on a set of possibilities. He asserts:

The communication presumes all elements together are presented, and the information received through a particular message is dependent on the set that such message provides. The information transmitted is not intrinsically the property of a single messenger. (1971, p. 157)

THE CONCEPT OF LEVELS

When confronted with an ambiguous message, a person tends to select, among all possible meanings, two that are antithetical or contradictory. Then, in order to satisfy the need to find solely unequivocal meaning, he or she will choose only one of the two meanings identified as contradictory. From these observations the fact may be derived that ambiguity and contradiction in others' behaviors *always* allow a choice, whether right or wrong, among the many possible ways in which the relationship can be understood. We stated *always*, but is it really possible to make a choice in every circumstance? In order to respond correctly to this question, it is necessary to examine the concept of *levels*.

We have seen how the concept of levels derives from the profound transformations in modern logic. The relevance of levels, in a systems perspective, became critical for family therapists to recognize and comprehend in their work with families of schizophrenics. Attempts to understand these types of families, while limited to only one level of significance, have proven to be totally inadequate. A schizophrenic family, for example, is capable of speaking of totally irrelevant matters over long periods of time and for a good number of sessions. This can continue despite persistent efforts on the part of the therapist to introduce more pertinent subjects. Remaining on the content level and trying to change the present content to another that is considered more meaningful will correspond to the impossible task of obtaining a clear and open way of communicating in a family terrified of clear, open communication. On the contrary, if we consider other levels of meaning, we will easily discover how even a very limited form of communication can make sense.

In the Grossi family, speaking about the weather was the preferred activity during the family therapy hour. Any other issue raised by the therapist was accepted only for a very short time, then, easing in with a very subtle passage, the family would resume its discussion about weather conditions.

They showed an incredible ability to extend this subject into an infinite number of possible directions: rain, snow, hail, clouds, sunny skies, humidity, and so on, were combined together from time to time, as needed, in varying degrees. In the process, past, present, future, and all the possible causes and consequences of weather conditions were thoroughly explored.

After a long discussion with his supervisor, it was suggested to the therapist that he look carefully into the implied levels of communication that existed beyond the subject of weather. The therapist later reported that he was finally able to understand the family and to see how at one level, while they were speaking of their ideas and feelings about weather, on another level they were speaking about their relationships with each other.

This dramatic shift in the therapeutic process took place when the therapist began to respond simultaneously to the different levels of meaning in the family and to understand the underlying family dynamics and conflicts, which were revealed while discussing apparently irrelevant issues. This is evident in the following transcript excerpt:

> *Mother:* Another week with bad weather like this and I'll go crazy. I really can't stand it.
>
> *Therapist:* You are the one in the family that can least tolerate bad weather?
>
> *Mother:* Well . . . my son is exactly like me. He suffers a lot on unpleasant days.
>
> *Therapist:* And what about the other family members?
>
> *Mother:* My husband doesn't care at all; he spends the day in the office, so I think he doesn't realize if it is raining or not.
>
> *Father:* I really don't care, as long as when I come back home the house is warm. I hate to feel cold in the winter, but my wife very often doesn't turn on the heat. She says it's because she wants to save energy.
>
> *Mother:* He doesn't feel cold in his office even when it snows, and they never use much heat there.
>
> *Therapist:* What makes you feel warmer in the office even on the colder days?
>
> *Father: (looking nervously out of the window)* Today it is a very foggy day, and it's impossible to see clearly.
>
> *Therapist:* Yes, and I have learned from my

own experience, that when it is like this,
it is better to stop the car and not drive,
or if I must, to drive slowly and carefully.
Mother: But sooner or later the fog will disappear and then it will be possible to see
everything clearly again, even things
that, before, could not be seen.

Confronted with such complex interactive patterns, the
recourse to multiple levels of understanding and their
types has proven to be a necessity.

Many works that have dealt with the idea of levels
have often neglected, unfortunately, to state clearly
which type of level was being considered. For this reason, the concept of levels has often been misunderstood.
The word "level" has an inherent vagueness and several
possible meanings. The types of levels most frequently
referred to in current literature are:

1. Communication levels
2. Coding levels
3. Content/relation levels
4. Organizational levels
5. Structural levels
6. Logical levels

Since using these different categories without clear
distinction has generated and continues to generate confusion, we will look briefly at the main characteristics of
each.

Communication Levels

This type of level carries the greatest risk of imprecise description. Within this type both the abstract and the concrete have been described and, more frequently, the verbal and nonverbal levels of communication. This very common error in description comes from a mistaken consideration of verbal and nonverbal communication. In themselves, these do not belong to different levels but are simply transmitted along diverse channels, as Sluzki and Ransom (1976) correctly explain:

> In retrospect, it is now clear that our efforts to consider in dialectic terms the correlative nature and the reciprocal influence of communication channels extend our discussions to the problem of communication levels, with respect to those which were not appropriate. (p. 320)

The idea of level necessarily implies that of hierarchy, and it is not possible to think that one channel is superior to the other.

Coding Levels

We refer here to the analogic and numeric (or digital) codes. The analogic code is of the continuous type, while the numeric consists of discrete elements. These elements are fully distinct and separate from each other by intervals that take on a notable importance for the significance transmitted by this type of code.

It is not possible, even in this case, to order hierarchically these two types of codes. Both codes, in fact, allow the sending or receiving of an infinite number of messages, and they complement each other. To be more precise, it should be stated, however, that the analogic code has a number of infinite possibilities of an order definitely higher in respect to the numeric code.

Human beings have developed very sophisticated digital coding systems such as layers, numbers, Morse code, and so on, because complex organizations necessitate this form of communication which is by definition less ambiguous than the one transmitted by the analogic code. When human beings are under pressure, or anxious, they usually prefer to use the digital code because it is more reliable and easier to understand. This explains why the more an interpersonal relationship contains emotional involvement, the greater is the tendency to translate analogic messages into the digital code.

The use of analogic and numeric codes does not, in itself, give rise to paradoxes. Nevertheless, in human relationships very serious problems connected with the process of translation from one code to the other can develop. This is particularly true when strong emotional commitment and/or expectations make a correct translation extremely difficult. The following case offers a clear example of this difficulty:

> Renato and Wilma married with very little knowledge about a sexual relationship; neither had had any previous sexual experience. What they knew they had heard from friends and relatives, but even this for the most part was extremely limited.
> With so little information about the subject,

each of them derived some anxiety which extended to their wedding night—the moment they both believed would be the most beautiful and tender moment of their lives. Renato had heard that it is important to a wife that a man appear strong and sure of himself on his wedding night. He was afraid that if Wilma saw any hint of uncertainty or hesitation, she would realize his lack of experience. Wilma was told that the first sexual experience could be painful and she was frightened by the idea that Renato might be forceful and even violent.

Since neither of them had the courage to speak clearly about their fears, they both approached that first night with a sense of anxiety strong enough to interfere profoundly with understanding of the analogic message and its translation into a digital communication code. When Renato's overall behavior was directed toward communicating "I'm strong and secure," Wilma, conditioned by her fear, translated it into "I'm violent," and when Wilma became frightened, Renato translated her analogic behavior into "I know you're not sure of what you are doing."

Upon closer examination of these premises we see that they were derived, first, from the fact that Renato began acting very determinedly and aggressive as soon as the couple was alone in the bedroom. He started to undress Wilma without any preliminary acts of tenderness or affection, and she considered this a confirmation that he could really be forceful and violent. Therefore, she became tense.

Renato felt her tension but translated it into indications that Wilma discovered how insecure he was and, so, he decided to be even more aggressive and literally jumped on Wilma. She was terrified and tried to stop him, but the more she tried, the more he wanted to demonstrate how strong and expert he was. Ultimately, he tried to have sex against her will, and she started to scream and punch him.

Given this difficult situation, he failed to have an erection; when she commented, "You are not the man I thought you were," he took this to be the final proof that Wilma discovered his lack of experience, which left him feeling very frustrated. Attempting to save face, he began blaming her for not being sexually attractive.

Since that painful "infernal night," not only was the couple unable to have any more sex, but they didn't speak at all about any sexual issues for more than three years until they decided to have a child. This wish brought the couple to therapy.

In addition to the analogic and numeric, other codes also exist that are a part of levels and that are typical of human communicative skills. The *iconic* code uses concrete figurations, and the *metaphoric* code is based on abstract figuration. Since they are the products of an "ad hoc" combination of very well-integrated analogic and numeric elements, these codes are at a higher level than either the analogic or the numeric. Finally, it is important to remember that, with respect to the above-mentioned communicative levels, any coding level will always result in a higher level. In effect the code is, by definition, a metalanguage consisting of rules that make the language understandable.

Content/Relationship Levels

While it is not totally correct to speak of communication levels (we have seen that they should more appropriately be called channels), it is proper to speak of levels of content and relationship. The level of relationship is, of course, superior to that of content. In fact, while the latter simply contains information, the former provides information about information.

Organizational Levels

Organizational levels are levels of hierarchy bound to the distribution of power in any given system or family, in which there are representatives of different generations or power. Organizational levels can often be violated in dysfunctional families and institutions, as the following case demonstrates:

> In the Giulini family, the generational line between the parents and the children has been perceptively altered. It clearly separates the parents and two older sisters on one side and Lino, the 17-year-old son, on the other.

Some time ago, Lino developed some strange compulsive behaviors. The rest of the family obliges him by accepting what he does and by trying to follow all that he orders them to do. Lino doesn't want any food to be wasted, so each family member must finish all the food at every meal, not leaving even a crumb in their plates. Sometimes he will even attempt to order his parents to lick their plates to be sure the food is completely gone. Pieces of paper and other useless objects such as corks, cans, empty cracker or cereal boxes, and so on, must be saved in special bags, and this is done as part of a very precise ritual every evening.

In organizational terms, Lino's symptomatic behavior has induced a violation of the generational hierarchy in the family. A young boy has now assumed an incongruous parental position with respect to his parents and sisters. The Giulini case is an example of a serious system dysfunction but it is not, in itself, a paradox.

Structural Levels

A system is formed on the basis of determined structural characteristics, which allow one to identify the various structural levels. Thus, we have at the higher level the suprasystem and the supra-suprasystem, and so on, and, conversely, at the lower levels, the subsystem, and the sub-subsystem, and so on.

Logical Levels

This level category is generally connected to the Theory of Logical Types, developed by Russell (1908), but introduced earlier by Peano and Schroeder. The purpose of the theory was to avoid "the vicious circle fallacy" (Russell, 1908) that can arise when there is a violation of its basic principle, which states: "No totality can contain members identified in terms of itself." In order to respect this principle, every set that contains within itself a determined variable must not be a possible value of that variable.

The first logical level (*first type*) is composed of only terms or individuals. The *second type* is a set composed of individuals plus the relationships that bind them, and the *third type* is a set of sets of the second type, and so forth.

THE RECURSIVE CHAIN

Complexity

Not all of the types of levels we have just described can be positioned according to a simple order, such that one is at a higher or lower level than the other. At times we can find ourselves faced, instead, with a *complex* hierarchy.

In a complex hierarchy, the less complex level is not only found at a lower level, with respect to the higher, but is also contained by it. Each higher level is more complex than the lower (in that it contains the lower) but is less complex than the still higher level which, in

TABLE 1
Type of Levels and Their Characteristics

TYPE OF LEVELS	TYPE OF HIERARCHY	POSSIBILITY OF PARADOX
Communication	none	no
Coding	simple/complex	no/yes
Content/relationship	simple	no
Organizational	simple	no
Structural	complex	yes
Logical	complex	yes

turn, contains it. When we have a complex hierarchy it is, in a way, similar to the game of Chinese boxes. The higher level, which is also the more complex, contains within it all the less complex levels.

The logical and the structural levels are ordered on a basis of an increasing degree of complexity, in which the higher (more complex) levels contain all the lower (less complex) levels. Both the logical and structural levels are nothing but different forms (logical in the first case and pragmatic in the second) of one and the same aspect: the *hierarchy of complexity.*

The complexity is characterized from (a) the emergent characteristics, which are the qualities that emerge in the transition from one level of complexity to another level of superior or inferior complexity (and these qualities were not previously present as such before the transition, at either the inferior or superior level); and (b) from the bonds or negative emergences which are the qualities that are lost in the passage to the higher or lower level. These aspects are further explained in Morin (1983, pp. 136–137).

All the other levels, previously described, are ordered with respect to a type of *simple hierarchy*. The only exceptions are the iconic and metaphoric codes which, as we have pointed out, are of a higher complexity with respect to the digital and analogic codes of which they are composed.

Considering all the types of levels, only those ordered according to a hierarchy of complexity can lead to a true paradox. In fact, we have a paradox only *when one less complex term is formed in such a way (ambiguity) as to contain inside itself another more complex term that, in turn (contradiction), being more complex, contains it.* There will not be a paradox when a concept, a code, a relationship, or a system of major complexity contains in its entirety only simple or less complex terms.

The Stochastic Process

Without a hierarchy of complexity, a true paradox does not occur even when ambiguity and the contradiction that derives from it occur at the same level, or at levels ordered according to a simple hierarchy. In this case, instead, we will have a succession of events that lead to a *stochastic chain*.

A succession of events is defined as a random sequence when the events composing them appear to have an equal probability of taking place. This property of the events makes it practically impossible to predict their future behavior: by its nature, a sequence of this type does not produce any new information.

Nevertheless, a system has the possibility to operate on a random sequence through a series of trials and errors, a selective procedure, and a successive organization of the selected events that are then transformed into information. This process that leads to learning, or through reaching higher levels of complexity to evolution (see Bateson, 1976, p. 147), can be called a stochastic chain.*

Ambiguous concepts, messages, stimuli, and events of ambiguous nature evidently contain within themselves a series of elements of equal probability. When moving away from ambiguity, one progresses toward a contradiction. We then have the first phase of the selective process that reduces the series to only two antithetical elements that are considered equally probable. The selective process comes to a close when a choice is made between one of the two equally probable elements (trial). If the choice is found to be satisfactory, it will be maintained; otherwise, if unsatisfactory (error), it will be conveniently corrected (learning). Through the stochastic process, a transition from an uninformative sequence to one which is informative has been made.

The Recursive Chain

Each piece of information acquired in a stochastic process influences the following choice and assumes the form of a *recursive chain*. For example, a mother says to her son, "You are a little monster." But the content of

---

*The term "stochastic" is derived from the Greek "stochastikos," which means to take aim and shoot at the target (with the release of the arrow from the bow, or with a javelin) and indicates a progressive selection effected on a random sequence through trials and errors, each time more accurate.

this message is accompanied by another message about the relationship which, through an affectionate tone of voice and a look of pride and admiration, expresses the meaning, "You are wonderful." This creates an ambiguity that has become a contradiction between two possible yet opposite meanings contained within the message.

Since the contradiction involves two different levels (content and relationship), with the two levels ordered in a simple hierarchy, we do not have a paradox. Instead, we face a simple contradiction that can be easily resolved by the recursive chain that we have just described.

If the child did not have a similar previous experience and had not already learned to determine which meaning he must attribute to this type of message, he would eventually choose either one of the two alternatives. Then, if his choice reveals itself to be wrong, he will subsequently correct it. Whether right or wrong, a choice is always possible and, therefore, the recursive cycle (which will be explained in Chapter 4) allows the acquisition of information that can be utilized as learning in future experiences.

The recursive process is utilized as well by the therapist in formulating hypotheses when confronting ambiguous phenomena that take place in the family. If, for example, during a first session, a father has a slight tremor in his voice when he scolds his daughter for creating a mess in the therapy room, this ambiguous event can at first have a great number of meanings, all of equal probability. In order to make his or her hypotheses, the therapist then selects two antithetical meanings which can be attributed to this event:

1. The father has a position of authority in the family, but the therapist's presence makes him nervous.
2. The father wants to demonstrate a position of authority in front of the therapist because he knows he does not have this position but thinks he should.

Whichever of the two alternatives the therapist chooses for his or her first hypothesis, the ambiguity and the contradiction do not prevent the selection of elements that will initiate the recursive cycle, and that may confirm or disprove the chosen hypothesis. In any case, it can offer further information.

All of the ambiguity and contradiction that we have examined in this chapter are of the simple, not complex, type. Nevertheless, we must remember that even simple ambiguity and contradiction require a level of greater complexity in order to be resolved. As we shall see in the following chapter, when an incongruity occurs regarding the levels of complexity, certain phenomena take place, rendering the choice—at least as the concept of "choice" is usually understood—impossible.

CHAPTER 4

✦✦✦✦✦✦✦✦✦✦✦✦✦✦✦✦✦✦✦✦

THE REFLEXIVE CHAIN

"The distinction between cause and effect is valid only for particular cases; but when we consider these particular cases in their general connections with the rest of the universe, cause and effect merge, and they end up being universal actions and reactions where cause and effect together create a dance and what is an effect now, becomes cause elsewhere, or, in another moment, and vice versa."
—Frederick Engels, *Anti-Duhring*

CIRCULAR PHENOMENA

The interest in *circular phenomena* continually increases in the study of human behavior, and it is further motivated through the knowledge now available in cybernetics.

In addition to concepts commonly used, such as feedback, circular causality, and so on, others now exist which must be explored as well in order to avoid the misunderstanding and misuse that can sometimes generate confusion.

Feedback

Feedback is considered one of the most important mechanisms of regulation in a system; it intervenes both in

55

the system's modification (positive feedback) and in the stabilization (negative feedback) processes.

Feedback consists of a closed circuit where information leaving the system (output) connects with information that has previously entered (input). In this way, it can act retroactively on the input received by the system, thereby regulating its frequency and intensity. As an example, in the course of a conversation the reaction of others to whom we are speaking will induce us to raise or lower our tone of voice. We may also increase or decrease the tempo of our speech in order to be sure that what we say is perceived exactly as we intended.

As Dell (1982) notes: "What is fed back may cause the target variable to remain constant and, at the same time, may cause the system as a whole to evolve!" (p. 28). Therefore, the same feedback may have a negative (stabilizing) value within the system and a positive (change) value when considered within other systems. This aspect of feedback was previously noted by Ashby (1971):

> The concept of feedback, as it is commonly understood, is simple and natural in certain elementary cases, only becoming artificial and difficult to use when the interconnections between the parts become more complex. Therefore, in order to have an understanding of the general principles of the theory of systems dynamics, the concept of feedback is, in itself, inadequate. (pp. 72–73)

In accordance with the opinion of Ashby, we can say that feedback is a regulatory mechanism—simple, but not suitable to describe the complex interactions within a system. However, feedback proves itself to be useful when considering the system as a whole.

Feedforward

Feedback allows the system to appropriately modify its behavior on the basis of the response it receives. It is necessary, however, that the system knows how to recognize among these responses which must be considered useful feedback. That is, a mechanism for the selection of feedback must exist through which the system can decide from time to time which circuit must be activated.

This mechanism is *feedforward* and it has the principal function of anticipating possible external input, thereby preparing in advance the activation of the opportune feedback. Moreover, feedforward preestablishes the range of responses that the feedback can give as well as its minimum to maximum thresholds. Feedforward is, therefore, the regulator of the mechanisms of regulation or, we could say, the *meta feedback that regulates the feedback*.

If, for example, a listener demonstrates boredom, raising one's voice could prove to be inadequate feedback to regain the listener's attention. Instead, we could elect as feedback to address him or her with a direct question which would then require involvement. The feed forward circuit can also select from among other possible alternatives, for example, silence, a joke, a direct or indirect comment, and establish limits within which any one of these can be considered appropriate for the desired outcome.

Feedback and feedforward represent the natural way

of change and adaptation that the system possesses at any given moment of its history. To be more precise, they represent the way in which the system changes and the way in which the system changes its way of changing, respectively.

From a therapeutic perspective, to bring about change in a family system one must intervene on the feedback mechanisms. This change, however, will be more like a simple oscillation than a real evolution of that system and, after a limited variation of its prior behaviors, will continue to act in the same way as before.

Contrary to this, effective intervention on the feed forward mechanism determines a meaningful structural change in the system, that is, changing its way of changing. This type of change is destined to last for a long time and eventually will change the system history.

For example, if a therapist's intervention in a family with an anorectic girl induces the girl to eat properly that same evening (feedback intervention), this does not indicate that the girl will continue to eat and be cured of her anorexia. Instead, in this case, we have only a short-term oscillation, which may change the quantity of food that she will consume at that one meal, but it will not impact enough to affect her history or the family's history of which the anorexia is a part.

A feedforward intervention could be directed, instead, toward the way in which both the girl and her family consider food. If the intervention is effective, all family members will be able to stop perceiving food as the only way to communicate closeness, and they will no longer use food as a means to control each other. The entire family will slowly and steadily lose its "anorectic quality."

As can be seen, the feedforward circuit has notable importance in the system's behavioral choices, and it is unclear why it has been so little studied. Feedforward is a *closed circuit*, but *complex*, since it is composed of feedback that regulates feedback.

Loops

We are speaking here of a broad general term used to indicate the presence of the phenomenon of a circular course. In fact, we may have feedback loops, reflexive loops, and so on. An even more specific value was attributed to loops by Hofstadter (1979) who writes of "strange loops":

> The strange loop phenomenon occurs whenever, by moving upwards (or downwards), through levels of some hierarchical system, we expectedly find ourselves right back where we started. (p. 10)

Hofstadter's definition of the phenomenon actually corresponds to *reflexivity*, a concept which will be addressed further throughout this chapter.

Cronen, Johnson, and Lannaman (1982) distinguish, on the basis of the type of reflexivity, strange loops that are "problematic," that is, capable of causing pathology, and charmed loops, loops capable of charm and not at all problematic because they are endowed with the property of nonprovoking mutually exclusive interpretations. Charmed loops have, in the terminology of the authors, a "transitive quality." In their broader definition, loops always comprise closed circuits, but these can be either simple (feedback loops) or complex (strange loops).

Self-reference

Self-reference pertains to messages or propositions that make reference to themselves. As an example, when one writes in a letter "this letter . . .," a self-reference is indicated because the letter speaks of itself. The same is true for the message, "This is a message." With some couples, self-reference becomes a way of communicating without communicating. The members of this type of couple spend a great deal of their time discussing their way of interacting: it ends up in an endless (but not circular) theoretical interaction that prevents any intense involvement.

In these cases, self-reference becomes a sort of intellectual phobic avoidance or "the art of speaking without ever meeting." In one couple of this type, we found the following sequence:

Husband: I would like you to understand what I say, the way I understand what you say.
Wife: But I always try to speak to you with an awareness of the way you will understand me.

Sometimes this talking about talking can go on for hours, creating an incredible amount of intricacies and often serious problems in the relationship. Nevertheless, self-reference does not introduce, by itself, reflexiveness and paradox.

Self-reference may sometimes become confused with reflexiveness. However, this confusion can be justified only under particular conditions: a self-reference, if it does not meet with other circumstances that modify its structure, is only the premise of a possible phenomenon of the circular course. It is not, in itself, enough to determine a circular effect.

Circular Causality

Circular causality is a particular case of reciprocal causality. The latter consists of two simple linear causal connections that are direct in the opposite sense of one in respect to the other, as for example, A > B and B > A. If the two causal connections form an immediate repetitive sequence, we will have a *reversible causality*: A > B > A. If this reverse action takes place by means of a connection of successive causal events, it determines loops and cycles that are able to recur several times. We then have *circular causality* (see Figure 1).

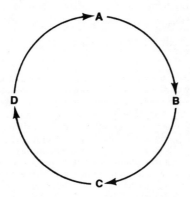

Figure 1. Circular Causality

Circular causality *is composed of a series of simple linear causal connections; therefore, circular causality does not eliminate linear causality* but is of a higher order in respect to these.* One can say, therefore, that circular causality consists of a complex level of epistemic knowledge based on the correlations that exist between simple causal connections. It is, then, a circular chain of events, both closed and complex. We identified circular causality as a "circular chain of events" but, actually, in our opinion it would be more correctly referred to as a *way to see* the circular chain of events.

Recursiveness

This is another term taken from mathematical logic that came into use in the 1930s. The concept was later extended to cybernetics and, more recently, to the behavioral sciences. In the behavioral sciences, the idea of a recursiveness has been well received but, unfortunately, it is utilized with so many diverse and contrasting meanings that the concept has become what Bateson (1972a) identified as "Dormitive Principles," tautological notions that do not result in any significance.

---

*Halbwachs (1984), starting with studies conducted at the Center of Genetic Epistemology of Geneva, indicates that the acquisition of the circular type of causality corresponds to a more advanced phase of an individual's psychological development. The research data shows that while the child around 7 or 8 years of age is in a position to recognize the presence of linear causal connections, he develops the conception of a process of circular causality only at about 13 to 15 years of age. The author concludes that the individual "initially requires a long phase at the level of simple causality, first learning to consider separately, and one at a time, the two unilateral moments of which the simple causality is formed. He is then able to grasp the correlation of the two elementary causalities that now can be seen together in a circular causality, richer, but of more difficult acquisition." (p. 113)

A number of meanings have been attributed to the term "recursivity," among which are, circular phenomena (in a broad sense), complexity, repetition, redundancy, retroaction, circular causality, reflexivity, and paradox. We prefer to use the term "recursivity" in a more restricted sense, closer to that originally conceived in modern logic. According to this point of view, a set is defined recursively enumerable when, starting with a limited number of departure points (axioms) and repeatedly applying well-defined rules, it is possible to generate, one after the other, all of its elements.

It is a "process," as Hofstadter (1979) correctly notes, "in which new things emerge from old things by fixed rules" (p. 152). Hofstadter emphasizes the fact that, according to this process, one moves from elementary presuppositions in order to arrive at conclusions always more complex and, at certain levels, perhaps even unpredictable. He compares the recursive process to that followed by human intelligence and uses that as a basis to hypothesize the possible development of artificial intelligence.

We use the concept of recursivity in the sense of *a process that starts from well-founded elementary presuppositions and arrives at complex conclusions, based on repetitions of well-defined rules.* Therefore, recursivity uses the repetition of rules in order to arrive at complexity. Keeney (1985) also states:

> The image of a circle is perhaps not the best way to picture a recursion because of the fact that we do not refer to its return in a time, and at an initial point of origin. Every recursive spiral implies a different starting point even if, in

terms of the model of organization, it is simply recycling. (p. 71)

Consider the following case:

> In the Neri family, the parents married when they were in their forties and soon they had Gianni, a very lively only child. From the very beginning, they felt that they were too old and too committed to their work to succeed in effectively raising and disciplining their restless child. They asked the mother's younger sister, Diana, to come to live with them and take over the job of parenting Gianni.
>
> Diana accepted, and for several years things seemed to go much better with her presence in the home, until one day when she announced that she would soon marry and move away. When Diana left, the Neris became desperate. Gianni began to misbehave both at home and in school and they still did not feel in control of his behavior.
>
> They then decided to ask for help from Luisa, Mr. Neri's mother, an energetic woman who was considered very strong natured. She came to their home every day for a year and took care of the young boy. When a serious family argument erupted over an inheritance from Mr. Neri's father, Luisa refused to continue to care for Gianni. She fully withdrew from any involvement in his upbringing.

Shortly after, the parents employed Fiorella, a 35-year-old nurse who lived next door to the family, to take Luisa's place. She was very cooperative and enthusiastic about her work with Gianni, until her husband felt she was so involved in taking care of the Neri child that she was neglecting her own family. Fiorella, with much regret, left the family at her husband's request. However, she did suggest to the Neris that, based on Gianni's difficult behavior, they should initiate family therapy.

Gianni's parents' feelings of inadequacy led to a recursive pattern of asking for outside help. This recursive pattern of continually applying the same solution to Gianni's problem behavior never did solve the problem. On the contrary, it only served to maintain it. Thus, a recursive pattern may lead to a good or poor adaptation, depending on a variety of factors. Nevertheless, even when it is dysfunctional, recursion does not necessarily imply a paradox.

The *recursive chain* that was presented in Chapter 3 can now be defined as *a sequence of events recursively generated*. It does not have a circular course; it may evolve instead toward positions of greater stability or complexity. It is, therefore, unjustified to identify it as a circular phenomenon or, even less so, as a closed circular phenomenon (which always returns to the departure point) or as a paradox. The recursive chain can produce circular phenomena or paradoxes only when it flows into the *reflexive chain*.

TABLE 2
Circular Phenomena and Their Characteristics

CIRCULAR PHENOMENA	TYPE OF CIRCULARITY	TYPE OF HIERARCHY
Feedback	circular/closed	simple
Feedforward	circular/closed	complex
Loops	circular/closed	simple/complex
Self-reference	circular but only when it takes place in two different complexity levels	simple/complex
Causality		
Simple	open/not circular	simple
Reciprocal	open/not circular	complex
Reversible	closed	complex
Circular	closed/repetitive	complex
Recursivity	open/not circular	complex
Reflexivity	closed/circular/ repetitive	undecidable oscillation simple/complex
Vicious circle	closed/circular	undecidable oscillation simple/complex

THE REFLEXIVE CHAIN

In *What is the Name of This Book?**, Raymond Smullyan (1978), professor of mathematical logic and author of some enjoyable books of riddles and paradoxes, presents the story of his first encounter with logic. Smullyan recalled that when he was 6 years old, his older brother Emile came into his room and said:

> "Raymond, today is April Fool's Day, and I will fool you as you have never been fooled before."
> "I waited all day long for him to fool me," reported Smullyan, "but he didn't." Late that night my mother asked me, "Why don't you go to sleep?" I replied, "I'm waiting for Emile to fool me." My mother turned to Emile and said, "Emile, will you please fool the child?" Emile then turned to me and the following dialogue ensued:
>
> > *Emile:* So, you expected me to fool you, didn't you?
> > *Raymond:* Yes.
> > *Emile:* But I didn't, did I?
> > *Raymond:* No.
> > *Emile:* But you expected me to, didn't you?
> > *Raymond:* Yes.
> > *Emile:* So I fooled you, didn't I? (p. 3)

---

*The title of Smullyan's book, *What is the Name of This Book?*, itself contains a question which leads to a reflexive circuit that can be interrupted only with the use of quotation marks, in a delimiting sense, to distinguish the question from the title, that is, What is the name of this book? "What is the Name of This Book?"

Later, in bed with the light off, Raymond continued to ask himself whether or not he had been fooled.

> On the one hand, if I wasn't fooled, then I did not get what I expected, hence, I was fooled. (This was Emile's argument.) But with equal reason, it can be said that if I was fooled, then I *did* get what I expected so, then, in what sense was I fooled? So, was I fooled, or wasn't I? (pp. 3–4)

Here is another example of reflexivity. Without proper limitations the dilemma, yes, no, yes, no, could continue indefinitely.

In order to give an account of how one develops a reflexive chain, we will examine the various passages that lead to this outcome. First, the statement, "I will fool you as you have never been fooled before," contains an *ambiguity* in the sense that whatever Emile meant by being fooled, nothing in particular was specified. Emile, then, left all possibilities open. Little by little, as time passes, the ambiguity transforms into the proposition of two *contradictory alternatives*: Was Raymond fooled, or was he not fooled?

At this point, we are caught in the *recursive chain*. In fact, if other complications do not enter, the answer could be yes or no (depending on the behavior of Emile), and everything would simply stop there. But Emile opened the route to the reflexive chain with the statement that he *had* succeeded in fooling Raymond because he had not fooled him. With this statement, the level of *complexity* comes into play.

The statement, "I will fool you as you have never been

fooled before," contains at least a double level of complexity:

1. It simply announces a future April Fool's joke; and
2. The announcement itself is already the April Fool's joke.

The *reflexive chain* is initiated in this way and persists with *self-reference*. In fact, the announcement of the April Fool's joke refers to itself (in a nonexplicit form).*

We have seen that self-reference is, in itself, a simple and noncircular phenomenon, but what if the self-reference refers to something that belongs to different levels of complexity? What if, as in this case, the announcement of an April's Fool's joke contains the April Fool's joke? When self-reference involves two levels of complexity, it generates *reflexivity*. We actually have the statement of an April Fool's joke that contains an April Fool's joke that contains the statement of an April Fool's joke, that contains . . . and so on.

It generates, therefore, an infinite oscillation between possible, diametrically opposite significances, and it develops into a reflexive circuit that is circular, closed, and repetitive. This circuit brings us again to the so-called "vicious circle," another link of the reflexive chain, and

---

*The self-reference, in this case, is deliberately not explicit in order to generate expectation. In reality, it is as if Emile himself was saying: "This is not an April Fool's joke, but only the announcement of an April Fool's joke," but this explicit statement would have made Raymond suspicious. In fact, in whichever of the two contradictory ways the ambiguous message could have been explicit, the same message would have lost the characteristics of ambiguity and of reflexivity. It would have been either true ("This announcement of an April Fool's joke is already the April Fool's joke") or false ("This is only the announcement of an April Fool's joke, it is not the April Fool's joke").

that link contributes to definitively close it. At this point, *an oscillation to infinity takes place between levels of complexity that renders the initial contradiction undecidable.* The April Fool's joke is an April Fool's joke only if it is not and is not an April Fool's joke if it is, and so on. Poor Raymond is said to have stayed awake most of the night attempting to escape this inextricable dilemma, and we have no idea how long he suffered from the pragmatic effects of the paradox. Certainly, the impasse was overcome at a higher level by Professor Raymond Smullyan, an amusing scholar of paradox.

We are now in a position to reconstruct the entire route that leads to the *reflexive chain* and to the vicious circle that produces the *undecidability* which characterizes paradox. Paradox always begins with a simple *recursive chain*. First, there is an *ambiguous term* (a statement, a message, an ambiguous relationship), which can hold many different possible meanings. From these, we arrive at a contradiction, which contains two possible yet opposite meanings, both equally probable. At this point, it is still possible to find a way out through a *stochastic process* which has the capacity to produce, by means of an initial random choice, information that will later influence future choices. If things proceed this way, we will have only a simple recursive chain that then leads to a *higher recursive order* (see Figure 2).

However, if the ambiguity is systematic in Russell's sense (whereby the possible meanings belong to various levels of complexity) and if the contradiction is also not a simple one but involves different levels of complexity, then the reflexive chain will begin. The contradiction, placed on two different levels of complexity, will give rise to a particular complex type of self-reference and

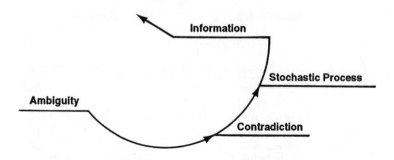

Figure 2. The Recursive Chain

bring about reflexivity. Since reflexivity does not have a way out, it produces the vicious circle that ultimately renders the meaning (of the term, the event, the relationship, etc.) undecidable and, therefore, ultimately produces the paradox.

The recursive chain no longer flows into a higher recursive order. Instead, it reflects upon itself at the same level from which it departed and produces *undecidability*. Since undecidability carries only unclear, vague, and obscure meanings, it is possible to arrive again at an ambiguity and to still run from the recursive chain to reflexive chain, causing an endless oscillation that cannot produce any further information (see Figure 3).

Once we arrive at the point of undecidability, we have finally reached the end of the journey which has permitted us to recognize the elements that constitute paradox as well as the reciprocal relationship of these elements. In other words, beginning with systematic ambiguity, then passing on to complex contradiction, self-

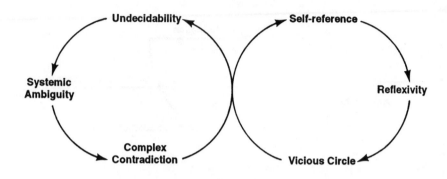

Figure 3. Paradoxical Reflexive Circuit

reference, reflexivity, and the vicious circle, we ultimately arrive at undecidability. This then completes the
paradoxical reflexive circuit that is composed of a recursive
chain flowing into a reflexive chain. *Paradox is, therefore,
a systematic ambiguity capable of producing undecidability by
means of an infinite reflexive oscillation among different levels
of complexity.*

Before concluding this journey, we will look at yet
another aspect, which is necessary in order to define
paradox in a simpler, more operationally useful form
and which will lead us toward further understanding of
the nature and origin of paradox in human relations.

THE ILLEGITIMATE TOTALITY

In the film *The Rear Window*, Alfred Hitchcock (1952)
recounted the story of a photographer who, temporarily

immobilized from a minor accident, spends the entire day observing from his window the movements of various people who passed back and fourth within his view. Notwithstanding a very modest set (in reality, the entire action takes place between the window and the adjacent courtyard), the film is meticulously executed and laden with suspense: the photographer succeeds in uncovering a crime and in unmasking the culprit, then finds he has placed himself in serious danger. However, the most fascinating aspect of the film is the stated intent of the author: that it was made as a metaphor of the movie world and of himself.

Hitchcock suggests that filmmaking is, in a certain sense, like a sickness; a form of voyeurism similar to that of the protagonist of the story who becomes more involved in the events he observes through others than in the experiences of his own life. Not even his charming girlfriend (played by Grace Kelly), who tries everything to reclaim his attention, can manage to succeed in bringing him back from the reality that exists for him beyond this window. Eventually, she herself will give up and become involved with the life of the courtyard. Only in this way is she able to reenter the protagonist's reality.

The film contains a unique and ingenious example of iconic metaphoric paradox.* The paradox is established on the ambiguity intrinsic in any artistic medium and on the contradiction at diverse levels of complexity: is it the film telling us about the movie world or is it the

---

*It is *iconic* because it contains concrete figurations built from the images of the film; it is *metaphoric* for its abstract figurations: the indirect representation of the movie world.

movie world that is telling us the story of the film? The self-reference is based on the fact that this is a film that describes, metaphorically, both itself and its own significance. In this way, we arrive at the reflexivity that becomes a vicious circle: the movie world tells about the film that tells about the movie world that tells about the film and so on.

The result of every attempt to decide if the film is telling us about the movie world, or if the movie world is telling us about the film, will be undecidable. It is, however, a very particular undecidability. It does not promote the unpleasant effect of entrapment typical of some pragmatic paradoxes. *The Rear Window*, like the iconic paradoxes found in the designs of Maurits Escher, elicits pleasant feelings and, perhaps thanks to their own paradoxical nature, they are considered masterpieces.

The result of this type of paradox is profoundly different from that of the paradoxes that have induced crises in logical thought or that have determined undecidable relationships in a family system. The difference is due to the *delimitation* that circumscribes the effect of these paradoxes, preventing them from creating an effect of *total* involvement.

The paradoxical reflexive circuit, contained as it is when presented within the confines of a movie screen or a picture frame, cannot effectively invade *all* the areas of life or relationships of an individual. This is because the paradoxes that are found in some forms of artistic expression, in games, in play, or in humor, are different from the logical and the pragmatic paradoxes. The former never produce a totality. The logical and pragmatic paradoxes, instead, always contain a *totality*.* In accordance with Russell, we can say that these latter types of paradox are an *assumption of illegitimate totality*.

In our opinion, one of the most enlightening ideas of the *Principia Mathematica* was that it captured the essence of paradox in a single concept. The assumption of illegitimate totality is, in fact, the nucleus of paradoxical structure. It reassumes within itself all the established elements of paradox that we have described, then completes them in a way that allows us to accurately evaluate the paradox's pragmatic impact (in the sense that the less limited the totality is, the more important this impact will be). Furthermore, this concept can offer an explicative model of the genesis of paradox in human systems and of the validity of paradoxical therapeutic interventions in dysfunctional family systems.

Totalities represent a concept much less flexible than the concept of "wholeness." In fact, as Aristotle (in *Metaphysics*, 1966) distinguished it, the totality is any ordered set, complete and perfect in its order, while the "whole" is any set of parts, regardless of their order.

CHAPTER 5

◆◆◆◆◆◆◆◆◆◆◆◆◆◆◆◆◆◆◆◆◆◆◆

THE ILLEGITIMATE TOTALITY

THE ORIGINS OF PARADOX IN HUMAN RELATIONSHIPS

We have seen that the assumption of illegitimate totality can, in reality, be considered identical with paradox, inasmuch as it contains all the same elements: systematic ambiguity, complex contradiction, self-reference, reflexivity, the vicious circle, and undecidability. But the term "illegitimate totality" has an important explicative value of its own in that it helps us to understand the actual nature of paradox and its pragmatic aspects.

Paradox arises as a consequence of an inappropriate totalization that tends to subvert a complex, logic, or pragmatic, hierarchy.*

---

*Many authors dwell upon the distinction between logical paradox and pragmatic paradox, considering them generally two different entities. In our opinion, it has to do with the same phenomenon: it assumes logical or pragmatic relevance based on the context in which it is being considered. That is, a logical paradox can have pragmatic effects if it is found in the context of human interaction (which is what happened in the example of the paradoxes utilized by Zeno to demonstrate the validity of his thesis and to make things difficult for his adversary). On the other hand, a paradox that produces a pragmatic effect does not lose its logical structure; it can always be recognized when examined under this aspect.

Yet, for what reason does a paradox, or an assumption of illegitimate totality, occur in human relations, and why can it produce seriously dysfunctional situations? (From here on, unless otherwise specified, both terms, paradox and illegitimate totality, will be used synonymously.) In our opinion, paradox is typical of the human species, which is inherently endowed with a number of qualities that can become an equal number of factors which predispose it to the assumption of illegitimate totality. These are (1) the inherent ambiguity of messages and of human relationships; (2) the search for an absolute truth; and (3) the capacity to predict.

The Inherent Ambiguity of Messages and of Human Relationships

The richness and the complexity that are part of human language render it an extremely versatile instrument, though frequently ambiguous and capable of simultaneously transmitting multiple and often contrasting meanings. As Wittgenstein (1980) notes:

> Language can disguise thoughts precisely in the same way that, by the exterior form of dress, one cannot conclude the form of thought about the dress. . . . (p. 21)

The capacity to conceal or disguise thought is only one of many reasons that can give rise to ambiguous messages.

Ambiguity can be *nonintentional* when one uses analogic signals which, by definition, do not have a well-defined significance. In reality, analogic language is the most conspicuous part of the human communicative modality (and actually the way of communicating in the animal kingdom). In fact, while it may be possible to avoid digital communication, it is not possible for man to realize an analogic "silence." Therefore, the well-known axiom—"it is not possible not to communicate" —would be more specifically correct as, "it is not possible not to communicate in the analogic mode."

At other times ambiguity can be *deliberately* sought after. For example, in forms of artistic expression and in humor, "Art," according to a paradoxical definition attributed to Picasso, "is a lie that makes us realize the truth" (Hughes & Brecht, 1979, p. 59).

Even *perturbations,* rumors, or other types of information occurring in this same context can render ambiguous the significance of a message that did not contain this ambiguity at the moment it was delivered. Beyond this, given the possibility of encountering ambiguity, the receiver of a message can be preconditioned, through his or her own expectation, to the point of *perceiving an ambiguity* that was not present at the time the message was transmitted.

Naturally not all messages are ambiguous or are perceived as such. This would make life impossible. Moreover, it is the ambiguous quality of some messages, sent or received, that allows us the expressive richness that is truly a human quality. Wittgenstein (1980) himself recognizes the importance of this richness: "The limits of my language determine the limits of my world" (p. 63). Human relationships have, in turn, an inherent ambiguity since they are the product of an interaction that varies continually, both as a function of the change

of the individuals who take part in it and as a function
of the evolutionary phases of the relationship.

The Search for an Absolute Truth

Bateson (1979) suggests:

> We humans seem to wish that our logic were
> absolute. We seem to act on the assumption that
> it is so and then panic when the slightest over-
> tone that it is not so, or might not be so, is
> presented.
>
>   In truth, a breach in the apparent coherence
> of our mental logical process would seem to be
> a sort of death. I encountered this deep notion
> over and over again in my dealings with schizo-
> phrenics, and the notion may be said to be basic
> to the Double Bind Theory that I and my col-
> leagues at Palo Alto proposed some twenty
> years ago. (p. 126)

In the influential opinion of Bateson, we can recognize
a tendency of human nature, most noticeable in schizophrenics, to consider reality in absolute terms based on
certain initial acquisitions which are retained forever
with total inflexibility.

Paradoxically, this search for logical and absolute
truth is one of the sources from which paradox most
frequently originates. "Rationalism," Kierkegaard said,
"is an irrational faith in reason" (1944, p. 54).

The consequence of these attitudes would be to sub-
divide the world into a series of true or false contra-

positions, expressed in the form of a more or less peremptory either/or. But this could not be utilized in the analogic field which does not contain discrete measures. Therefore, in this case the application of a logic of the either/or type produces an assumption of illegitimate totality. Naturally, this is not to say that ideas of the either/or type must be completely ruled out and replaced in every circumstance by a perspective of the both/and type. It would then simply be another illegitimate totality. Wilden and Wilson (in Sluzki & Ransom, 1976), who were the first to emphasize this aspect, state:

> On the one hand, as it appears, we have the traditional logic, dependent from the axiom of identity (non-contradiction); a logic that we know from experience will work *inside* any system we isolate in space and time. On the other, it seems, we find a logic of levels, differences, and paradox which contradict or negate the first. But this dilemma is merely an apparent one. Only from the perspective of analytics— which tends inexorably to neutralize or one-dimensionalize levels of relation by creating artificial (and imaginary) either/or symmetries, oppositions, and identities between propositions, states, and systems which actually differ in their logical typing—only from *within* this closed-system perspective can any opposition between two logics be assumed. (p. 273)

Further on, these same authors identified the dilemma created by this illegitimate totality in the ecosystemic epistemology:

In this, nevertheless, the ecosystemic epistemology provides us with a precious tool of analysis and criticism. Precisely because it is a multi-
dimensional logic of levels, in which either/or
disjunctions are subordinate to both/and connections, the ecosystemic epistemology sub-
sumes and includes the analytic perspective as
a complementary logical system of a lower logical type. To put it somewhat aphoristically: the
analytic and primarily digital epistemology depends on an impoverished and exclusionary
logic of *either* both/and, *or* either/or, whereas
the ecosystemic epistemology depends on a rich
and inclusionary logic of *both* both/and and ei-
ther/or. (p. 274)

Another way to be caught in assumptions of illegitimate totality founded on presumed absolute truth is
represented by what Levick (1983) identifies as "Paradoxes of Always-Never Land," that is, statements characterized by the use of the adverbs "always" and "never."
These are based on suppositions that do not allow exceptions. For example, the wife who says to her husband,
"You will never change," or the husband who accuses
his wife with, "You're always nagging me."

The Capacity to Predict

Human interactions are regulated by some principles
that have been defined as "strategic." At the root of this
definition is the capacity of human beings to anticipate

or predict the behavior of others and to act accordingly. Since this capacity for prediction belongs to *all* human beings, it means that the ability to predict others' behaviors makes their behaviors unpredictable.

Nigel Howard (1971) describes this phenomenon as one cause of the "breakdown of rationality" (p. 9). It utilizes a very eloquent metaphorical illustration. The author offers an example of two ships—a merchant ship and an enemy warship—which we have put into our own words:

> The merchant ship and the enemy warship are both approaching an island from opposite directions. Naturally, the two ships also have conflicting interests. The merchant ship would rather, for obvious reasons, avoid an encounter with the enemy warship, which would destroy it and, therefore, will try to take an opposite course, while the warship will do everything in its power to overtake the merchant ship in order to destroy it.
>
> The captain of one ship, therefore, will attempt to predict the route that will be taken by the captain of the other: to head toward the island respectively on the same or opposite side. Yet, if one supposes that both captains set out on their course with the information he presumes is correct, the prediction would be based upon an impossible expectation: the merchant ship would follow a different route than the warship, and the warship would follow the same route as the merchant ship.

As far as we are concerned, we can substitute the ships in Howard's example with an alcoholic husband who hides a bottle, and the wife who attempts to find it in order to prevent him from drinking. Even in this case, it is impossible that the predictions of both can be correct.

To render this game of interpersonal expectations even more complex, we can add higher logical levels that are sometimes brought into play by the person who tries to make the prediction: the person will not limit himself or herself to predict how the other would behave because he or she can also try to predict how the other would behave predicting how the person would behave, and then how the other would behave predicting how the person would behave predicting how the other would behave, and so on.

Or else, a totalizing presupposition encounters another totalizing prediction, as in the case of the couple described by Watzlawick (1965):

> A married couple are seeking therapeutic treatment for the wife's excessive jealousy, which makes life unbearable for both of them. It is revealed that the husband is an extremely rigid, moralistic person who takes great pride in his ascetic lifestyle, and in the fact that "I've never, in all my life, given anyone reason to distrust my word." The wife, who comes from a very different background, has accepted the complementary one-down position, except in one area: she is unwilling to forego her predinner drink, a habit which to him, as a teetotaler, is repulsive, and has been the theme of endless

quarrels practically since the beginning of their marriage. About two years ago, the husband, in a fit of anger, told her, "If you don't stop your vice, I'll start one of my own," adding that he would have affairs with other women. This did not bring about any change in their relationship pattern, and a few months later the husband decided to let her have drinks for the sake of domestic peace. At this precise point in time, her jealousy flared up, the rationale of which was and is: He is absolutely trustworthy, *therefore* he must be carrying out his threat to be unfaithful—that is, untrustworthy. The husband, on the other hand, is just as helplessly caught in the web of his paradoxical prediction, as he cannot convincingly reassure her that his threat was impulsive and should not be taken seriously. They realize that they are caught in a self-made trap, but see no way out of it. (p. 371)

This case fully introduces us to the interactive domain of paradox. We will see, in this domain, starting from the above-mentioned presuppositions (inherent ambiguity, search for absolute truth, capacity to predict), how paradox can develop in family relationships as well as in any other human system.

PARADOX IN RELATIONSHIPS

Beginning with the well-known Double Bind Theory (Bateson et al., 1956), a number of pathogenetic hypotheses based on the presence of paradox in human relationships has been elaborated. However, the interest for these hypotheses, which over the past decade have been highly upheld, is now very minimal. They have been almost totally replaced by the studies on therapeutic paradox, as evidenced in the many exhaustive reports on this topic (Seltzer, 1986; Weeks, 1991; Weeks & L'Abate, 1982).

We are convinced that, notwithstanding actual disinterest, the pathogenic hypotheses founded on paradox, while necessitating deep investigation and further research, still maintain their validity. Looking beyond this premise it is probable that a better knowledge of pathogenic paradox can help us to more clearly understand similarities and differences with respect to therapeutic paradox and, above all, its mechanisms of action that in large part still remain a mystery.

In the systemic view, many of the explicative models presented in the past have suffered from the effects of the uncertainty that prevailed in the field 30 years ago when the hypotheses on paradox were first proposed. Today we can say that an explicative model, in order to be consistent with the systemic point of view, should at least meet the following prerequisites:

1. To respect the principle of circular causality;
2. To be applicable both to the individual and to the system of which he or she is a part; and
3. To be coherent with the therapeutic procedures it proposes.

CIRCULAR CAUSALITY

This was one very neglected aspect in the past. The Double Bind Theory, for example, examined the effects of parents' behavior (attributing to them the responsibility for "scapegoating" the identified patient) on the children, but it did not examine the effects of the children's behavior on the parents.

INDIVIDUALS AND FAMILIES

From this point of view attention has often been given to the system or, more often, to one of its subsystems. Seldom has the individual alone been taken into consideration. In the few cases where the individual was considered, he or she has usually been thought of as the cause or the victim of a dysfunction in the system, as implied by such terms as "schizophrenogenic mother," "peripheral father," and "scapegoat." In other cases, the concept of the individual has been presented in opposition to the concept of system, rather than as one of its integrative components.

COHERENCE WITH THERAPY

As far as this aspect is concerned it must be stated that the relationship between pathogenic paradox and therapeutic paradox has been treated only briefly in the literature. This aspect will be treated more extensively in the following chapters.

We will now examine how the illegitimate totality hypothesis meets these criteria: circular causality; individuals and families; and coherence with therapy. The presuppositions of which we have spoken in the preceding paragraphs constitute the premises necessary, though not sufficient, to determine an assumption of illegitimate totality. In order to understand how these presuppositions lead to the illegitimate totality, we will use an example given by Jules Henry (1973), which offers a clear description of the process:

> If a man says "I love you" to a woman, she may wonder whether he means it, whether he loves her, how much he loves her, whether he will love her next week or next year, or whether this love only means that he wants her to love him. She may even wonder whether his love includes respect and care, or whether his love is merely physical. "I love you" is surely an ambiguous message. The woman may come to the conclusion that his idea of love is not hers and that the kind of love he has to give would not make her happy. So in spite of his caresses and in spite of the fact that she enjoys the man, the woman refuses to marry him and breaks off. (p. 191)

The ambiguous message "I love you," which Henry examines for many possible meanings, is analyzed by the woman who attempts to find in it an absolute meaning. The woman, however, does not limit her search to only one absolute meaning. In addition, she attributes to it a value that, without exception, she extends to the entire relationship. Moreover, the capacity to make predictions induces her to consider the partner's future behavior and to regard it as unquestionably predictable in the future. Thus, for an individual who processes the information received in terms of an illegitimate totality, every *hypothesis* is unavoidably transformed into an *axiom that does not need to be demonstrated.*

In the previous example we have been faced only with the way in which an individual develops an illegitimate totality. The perspective through which the example was presented has demonstrated only the linear aspect of this development. After having examined it from the individual and linear points of view, we will now look at illegitimate totality through an example which will allow us to observe it in an interactive situation and in the light of a circular perspective.

> Bianca and Mario have been married for some time. One evening, while going to bed, Mario says to Bianca, "Bianca, I want to make love." Bianca, perhaps only because she is tired, answers honestly, "I really don't want to." Mario is surprised and cannot come up with an explanation that he can accept, and so comments, "You *must* want to."

This statement indicates that Mario considers desire (necessarily spontaneous) a sort of obligation, something that must always be present. This totalization can have no consequences on the receiver's behavior if the message is not also perceived in a totalizing way. Therefore, a paradoxical definition, or injunction, has a pathogenic effect only if the receiver attributes to it an absolute value.

The "prohibition to escape from the field" (Bateson et al., 1956), which was originally identified as a necessary ingredient of the "double bind," must, in our view, be reconsidered from this perspective. It is not the sending of the message that prevents the "victim" from escaping the pathogenic effects of the injunctions. Rather, it is the totalizing form of the interpretation that the recipient gives to the illegitimate totality made by the other.

A tragic demonstration of this is the Greek inscription which was spoken of in the first chapter. According to the inscription, the logician Philetas of Cos dedicated himself totally to the attempt of resolving the Paradox of The Liar, neglecting his own health to the point of death. Therefore, a paradox does not have a pathogenic effect if, in turn, the one who receives it does not assume it as a totality, while even an innocuous logical paradox can have a profound pragmatic effect if the receiver considers it as a totality.

In reality, a true pathogenic paradox is that which originates from two (or more) totalizations that meet. From this perspective we can see both the participation of each individual and the importance of their relationship in the formation of pragmatic paradoxes. We also can then understand how single linear causality contributes to form a process of reciprocal causality.

In the case we have described, Bianca could have simply left everything as it was, perhaps even explaining her different point of view; then the following night she could have approached Mario with a smile on her lips that would clearly state her desire to still make love with him. If, instead, Bianca attributes to Mario's words the weight of a statement that brings their entire sexual relationship into question, then all of his subsequent behavior in this area will be conditioned by this assumption. A paradoxical vicious circle could develop which will then involve not only Bianca but Mario as well.

In fact, if Bianca now wants to make love with him, considering his statement as an absolute truth, she will think that her behavior is only performed as a response to his demands. In order to meet his expectation, that she *must want* to, she should feel a genuine desire which, in order to be truly genuine, should not be a response to his request. If her desire is not a response to her husband's request, then it is not a genuine desire because a genuine desire is what he requested. Even Mario is no longer in a position to decide if Bianca makes love with him because it is truly her desire or because he requested it.

It could now be said that at least the sexual area of their relationship had become undecidable. Neither of them is in a position to decide if their sexual relationship is spontaneous or obligatory, and this undecidability can eventually be the source of symptomatic behaviors.

In addition, a relationship of a paradoxical type tends to activate further paradoxes. If Mario wishes to change the situation, he will begin to refrain from taking the initiative, expecting that this will facilitate a demonstration of spontaneous interest on her part. Bianca could then, noticing that something has changed in Mario's behavior, ask him to pursue the initiative. But if Mario accepts Bianca's request to pursue the initiative, it will no longer be his initiative. If, instead, he does not respond to her request, this will, in reality, be his initiative and, therefore, without even wanting to, he will end up obeying.

Mario, therefore, can only obey if he disobeys and can only disobey if he obeys. Once again, we have the vicious circle in which it is possible to recognize, through the presence of contradiction and self-reflexivity, the nature of pragmatic paradox.

As we have seen, however, what better characterizes the pragmatic paradox is the assumption of illegitimate totality. "You *must* want to" implies that among all the behaviors he can request, spontaneous ones (something which cannot be requested) are also included. This, therefore, determines the assumption of an illegitimate totality. On the other hand, Bianca's request, directed toward achieving more initiative from Mario, is based on the erroneous presuppostion that, among all possible suggestions, can also be included the suggestion of taking initiative (not realizing that initiative cannot be suggested).

In both cases, an illegitimate totality is assumed because some elements, which presuppose an entire class, are considered as terms of that class.

An important aspect of these transactions is that their order could be reversed without modifying their effect. There is little actual importance in whether "You must want to" or "You should take the initiative" was said first. Once stated, the error tends to self-perpetuate and to provoke still more errors. In addition, whichever person first makes the request, it does not necessarily imply an intent to hurt the other. In fact, with the collaboration of the other, each makes the relationship undecidable. They limit their own and each other's alternatives. Neither Bianca or Mario know for certain whether the sexual behavior of Bianca is, or is not, spontaneous and whether Mario takes, or doesn't take, the initiative.

The previous case is a description of a dyadic interaction in which the encounter of different totalities creates a paradoxical relationship. In the family system this *convergence* (and *divergence*) of totalities becomes more complex. The following chapter contains a more detailed description of how paradox develops in a family system.

CHAPTER 6

PARADOX IN THE FAMILY SYSTEM

AMBIGUITY AND UNDECIDABILITY
IN THE SYSTEM

It is important to make a distinction between ambiguity and undecidability. It is not at all uncommon for these two concepts to be used synonymously. In the field of human communications, *ambiguity* consists of presenting, simultaneously, a number of different meanings. This characteristic makes ambiguity an indispensable instrument for human beings to modulate their expression of complex affectivity. Ambiguity's presence can sometimes stimulate interpretation problems, but it is unlikely that ambiguity, by itself, could generate true pathology.

During a mother's visit to the hospital to see her son, who is recovering from a recent psychotic episode, she presents the son with behaviors that may be interpreted in many different ways: she is not congruent in that she expresses happiness through words while manifesting a cool and distant nonverbal attitude. In spite of the fact that some of the son's interpretations of his mother's behaviors may be unpleasant, he is, nevertheless, in the position to choose from among them the one that to him seems most probable. Inasmuch as he may be upset or hurt by his conclusions—which may be correct or incorrect or later modified or corrected by subsequent experience—this choice will not prevent him from making other choices in his ongoing relationship with his mother. Up to this point, the sequences of behavior remain within the recursive chain, which always permit further levels of learning to take place.

Undecidability is, in contrast, the pragmatic effect of a particular choice (the assumption of an illegitimate totality) that makes successive choices impossible and, usually, incorrectable. In this case, using the previous mother and son example, the son would not simply think, "I do not understand my mother's feelings," but could think, and subsequently say to her, "I never understand anything." This illegitimate totality alarms the mother who then responds, "But dear, you always understand everything." Both statements contain an illegitimate totality since they do not place any limitation to understanding and, respectively, to not understanding.

If either mother or son had placed some limitation to their statements, as, for example, "*At this moment* I don't understand anything" and "But dear, you usually understand *my feelings*," the paradoxical nature of the statement would have been eliminated. Instead, given the way the statements were presented, undecidability was initiated. In fact, if the son's statement is true, that he never understands anything, then he cannot even understand that he doesn't understand. His statement, therefore, is false. If his statement is false, then the mother's statement is true. Yet, if the mother's statement is true that the son always understands, then she has to give him credit for understanding, even when he states that he never understands; therefore, the mother's statement is false. However, if the mother's statement is false, then the son's statement is true . . . and so on.

Paradox, therefore, does not produce immobility but an infinite oscillation that makes both a point of view and its opposite appear probable. A paradox can satisfy contrasting points of view simultaneously and, given its undecidability, is difficult to prove false.

For this reason, as was stated earlier, each individual's hypothesis transforms itself into an axiom. Whoever formulates the axiom considers it to be already perfectly demonstrated and is, therefore, not in a position to correct it. Paradox, then, leads to a continuous oscillation from yes to no and, therefore, annuls the distinction that is necessary to effectively send and receive information. Since it produces an infinite oscillation, it completely eliminates all spatial-temporal parameters.

Not being consciously aware of the errors they make, the persons involved in an illegitimate totality will behave like the player, of Von Neumann, who cannot go beyond zero learning since, as Bateson (1972b) observed: "He may, for good reason, elect to make random moves or explorative moves, but he is, by definition, incapable of learning by trial and error" (p. 285).

CONVERGENCE (AND DIVERGENCE) OF TOTALITIES

We have seen how paradox is initiated in an interpersonal relationship of which two or more persons are a part. Of course, even a single individual can assume an illegitimate totality, but this assumption usually becomes a stable pattern only when reinforced (convergent totality) or contrasted (divergent totality) by other types of totalities. Totalities tend by their nature to develop in totalizing contexts, and within this context they can produce new totalities and/or bind themselves to other preexisting totalities.

The illegitimate totality must necessarily be nourished by other totalities; in their absence it will lose its source of endurance and tend to extinguish itself. This observation points toward a possible therapeutic modality of pathogenic paradox. In a system, therefore, the illegitimate totalities tend to stabilize themselves reciprocally, even when they are in obvious contrast. As we shall now see, this is due to some characteristics that they have in common:

> Some months ago, Elena began to exhibit a particularly bizarre and unexplainable behavior. She would run out of her house, completely undressed, and she would furiously fight her parents when they tried to stop her, insisting they were the cause of her behavior. Elena fully blamed them for not having taught her "how to face life" and continuously complained, "You won't allow me to be independent." Her mother claimed that she could partly understand the way Elena felt and, in fact, said to her: "You must make the effort to be independent." Elena's younger sister, who had already moved away from home to live with a friend, fully supported the mother's position. In con-

trast, the father who had always sympathized with Elena, said, "Elena must be left alone to decide for herself."

In a stable interactive system with rules, some members present *convergent totalities* that, in turn, may diverge in a more or less conflictual manner from the totalities presented by the other members. Finally, another member of the system can develop a peculiar form of totality (*mediating totality*) that seems to have the specific function of reconciling the other contrasting totalities.

This peculiar type of illegitimate totality, which almost always assumes the aspect of a symptom, is the one that is usually carried by the so-called "identified patient." From the effects of the behavior of the identified patient on the other members of the system, and conversely, by the effects of the others' behavior on the identified patient, one could say that the system acts as if this person represents the entire system, as shown in the following case.

A short time after her marriage, Teresa, who had lived her entire life in the small southern village where she was born, came with her husband to live in a large city in the north. Some months later, the husband agreed to Teresa's request that her parents, who lived alone in the country, come to live with them. Within a very short time in this new enlarged system, a conflict began to emerge from the presence of two contrasting totalities. According to the parents, bound to a cultural belief that a woman should be a full-time homemaker, Teresa "must choose to stay at home." According to the husband, who expected her to offer economic help, Teresa "must be free to go to work."

The choice between the *divergent totalities* of the parents and the husband would force Teresa to displease one or the other; to avoid this, Teresa *chose not to choose.* She developed a serious form of agoraphobia, which prevented her from leaving the house and, thus, reconciled, without upsetting anyone, the paradoxical demands that were placed upon her. It satisfied the husband: he believed that as soon as she was well, she would be able to go out to work as he wanted. It also satisfied the parents: since she was sick, she would remain in the house, as they wanted.

PARADOXICAL BELIEFS

The fact that paradoxes are often presented in the form of concise injunctions must not lead us to think that the essence of paradox consists in a single phrase, and that it is only this one phrase that can make undecidable the complex relationships which characterize a dysfunctional system. Analogously, as we will see, a therapeutic paradox cannot be built on a prescription only.

Pathogenic paradox can sometimes be expressed through phrases such as, "Be spontaneous" or "You must not listen to me." In reality, these phrases are no more than the product of a series of *beliefs* from which comes the assumption of illegitimate totality.

These beliefs are not recognized on the basis of a single phrase only but on a series of related behaviors, attitudes, and expectations, from which emerges a totalizing view of all relationships that exist within the system and with the outside world. In the previous chapter, we examined the premises that make possible an assumption of illegitimate totality. We will now look at the beliefs and identify the corresponding paradoxes that feed this illegitimate totality: these beliefs are violations of the complexity principles.

The Relationship Paradox

In the members of a system in which pragmatic paradox predominates, one can easily recognize a tendency to think of one part as the whole and, in particular, to *consider one part of the relationship as the entire relationship.* The definitions, injunctions, and predictions of others' behaviors which take place in this type of system: indicate the shared belief that a single individual, a single interactive exchange, or even a single message, can contain all relationships, an entire relationship, or an entire area of the relationship.

In fact, paradoxical definitions, prescriptions, and predictions pertain to (in the order of decreasing seriousness):

1. All the relationships;
2. The entire ongoing relationship; and
3. An entire area (usually the one that is considered most important) of the ongoing relationship.

For example, if a wife says to her husband, "You never take initiatives," her statement indicates a totalization that includes the absence of initiative by the husband in all of his possible relationships. This statement can, instead, be limited to only one relationship if the wife says, "You never take the initiative with me," or it may apply to only one area of behavior within the context of their relationship, as in the statement, "You never take the initiative in our sexual relationship."

The complementary (and totalizing) response of the husband could be of this type, "You must tell me what you want me to do." Or, if it is limited to only the relationship with the wife, "You must tell me the thing I must do for you."

The Individuation Paradox

Paradoxes that take place in a stable interactive system always contain a *request for individuation* that is made from within the system to one of its members. The problem emerges from the erroneous belief based, in this case, on the myths of individuation, independence, autonomy (more and more diffused in an industrialized culture), and on the fear of interpersonal dependence.

Individuation and dependence are always combined and simultaneously present (even if in different proportions from phase to phase) in all of the family life-cycle phases. Therefore, since a certain level of dependence must usually be tolerated, a requirement of *total* individuation is evidently illegitimate. The request by the system that one individuate from the other must be appropriate to the developmental level reached by that individual.

If the process of individuation begins with ontogenesis

and, therefore, any biological entity would tend to be individuated from the exact moment it began to exist, even in smallest part, it is clear that the attempt to obtain individuation is justified from the moment of birth. The matter, at this point, is to establish to what extent this individuation can be considered legitimate with regard to the different phases of the life cycle, remembering that it is always necessary to tolerate a certain level of dependence.

From birth to completed individual maturation, the level of individuation grows to reach its maximum value in the adult. Throughout this same period, the necessity for dependence tends, correspondingly, to diminish. Individuation is realized for levels as well as for areas, that is, movement, locomotion, language formation, nourishment, sexual development, and so on.

When a mother requests that her son feed himself, since he has already reached the proper intellectual competence and motor ability, this request for individuation does not correspond to the assumption of a totality, as the child did not receive a totalizing injunction. The injunction is, instead, well defined and delimited: the legitimacy is given by the fact that, in that moment, the child is in a position to meet the request. If the injunction were to occur earlier, when the development reached at that moment did not yet correspond to the child's ability to accomplish it, a vicious circle could be determined that may render problematic the future acquisition of that given competence.

The child's refusal, or his failure, could have provoked in the mother an increasing insistence: it could provoke in the child a growing sensation of distrust of his own abilities, which could ultimately induce the mother to increase her efforts in order to obtain the desired result, and so on.

We are faced here with an erroneous belief that consists in *requesting an inappropriate and undefined level of individuation, or autonomy, that can produce a more or less serious delay in the reciprocal individuation between the individual and the system of which he is a part.* It is necessary to emphasize that, in reality, paradox that takes place in a family system is the result of a desperate attempt to obtain emancipation, even if this attempt is made in a way that produces an always more rigid bond and a strong dependence.

Ultimately, we must still remember that the individual, to whom the request for an inappropriate individuation is given, contributes to feeding the paradox of individuation with another illegitimate totality, which consists in requesting his or her individuation to the others. In essence, if we want to translate in the usual emblematic phrases the totalization process that takes place in the system and that is derived from an individuation paradox, we will have a paradoxical request which is usually directed to the identified patient such as, "You must individuate." The equally paradoxical response is, "You must allow me to individuate."

The Paradox of Exclusion

The belief that reality and, in particular, relationships with others are considered in either/or terms is well developed among the members of a system that produces pathogenic paradox.

The tendency to rigidly hold to an opinion and to

exclude every possible alternative leads members of these families to experience every possible encounter in their internal and external worlds with an attitude of continuous contraposition, inducing them to always take a position for or against something. This results in a series of absolute dichotomies: true-false, good-bad, sane-insane, capable-incapable, and so on; thus, all those who enter into relationships with this type of family tend to be drawn into dichotomous interactions. These systems, and their members, do not succeed in conceiving of the of "both-and" possibility.

The Paradox of Choice

The freedom of choice is a necessary premise in the elaboration and in the transmission of information. There is indeed a direct proportion between freedom of choice and quantity of information that can be processed by a given system. Bateson (1972b) has distinguished the diverse levels of learning as a function of the possibility of choice given to an individual:

In *0 (zero) learning*, it is not possible to make a choice. Consequently, it is not possible to make a mistake and, therefore, to correct it. In this form of learning, for every stimulus there follows a specific, and always equal, response.

An example of an interaction in which 0 learning occurs, is the case of an alcoholic husband who promises to stop drinking to the wife who threatens to leave. Then, as soon as the crisis appears to have passed, the husband returns home drunk again. In a short time, he promises that he will never again do anything like this, and the wife again is convinced to stay. Neither of them is in a position to correct their responses, and the situation tends to repeat itself, even though it is unsatisfactory to both.

In *Learning 1*, it is possible to choose between a series of alternatives and, therefore, corrections that are rendered necessary can take place when the previously chosen alternatives are proven wrong.

The son who, after a number of negative experiences, decides to stop taking sides either with the father or the mother when they argue, and the parents who ultimately realize that when they do not seek the boy's support in their arguments are able to negotiate their conflicts with a greater likelihood of success represent an example of Learning 1.

In *Learning 2* (or "Deutero-learning"), one does not limit oneself to choosing between different alternatives within a given set. Instead, one chooses between different sets of alternatives, and from these, a new choice can be made. In other words, in Learning 2, one is in a position to change Learning 1 or to transfer it to other contexts. It is presumable that, at this level, those beliefs (founded on the preceding experience) that guide the behavior of the individual in his or her present, and/or future relationships with others, are created and consolidated.

The boy who, after having learned to avoid any involvement in the arguments between his parents, decides to resume this type of behavior later in life with his colleagues at work, is again utilizing this type of learning. Analogously, the parents, likewise, can extend their learning from this same experience by no longer including their families of origin in their disputes. Hence, both can take learnings from one experience and at some future time utilize it in different contexts.

Learning 3 consists of a change in the process of Learning 2 and indicates, therefore, the choice of a new process of making choices, which corresponds to the possibility of using different modalities for building one's own beliefs. Bateson states that this type of learning is rare and difficult to attain, even for human beings, the only beings having the capacity to achieve it.

Bateson (1972b) further emphasizes that Learning 3 can augment Learning 2 but can, paradoxically, also reduce it. He adds: "We shall see later, that to demand this level of performance of some men and some mammals can be pathogenic" (p. 293). We hold these considerations made by Bateson regarding Learning 3 as very important because, in our view, they are the key to understanding the "paradox of choice": an assumption of illegitimate totality that is at the basis of severe forms of pathology.

The totalizing belief that triggers a paradox of choice is bound to the idea that one can prescribe or induce Learning 3 in others. Probably, since the beginning of time, the idea of being able to change Learning 2 among our own kind was one of the major aspirations of man. In a family system or a couple, the importance of this goal is increased in intensity by the reciprocal affective involvement of the individual members.

At times, this attempt to modify the choices of the other becomes the ultimate priority, and it is not rare to encounter marriages that were established from the beginning with this expectation. This is demonstrated in the following case:

When Julia married Arnaldo she knew that he was shy and introverted. She had never been attracted to this type of man, preferring those who were more outgoing and sociable. Arnaldo was exactly the opposite, which Julia knew, from the first time they met. "I'm sure he'll change into the kind of person I need," she told herself, "because I'll show him how to enjoy himself with others. We'll have friends over often, and when he sees how happy he can feel, he'll just naturally become more outgoing and extroverted."

Of course, as almost always happens, this expectation leads to disappointment when compared with what actually takes place. The same situation can occur in a family system between parents and children who tend to reciprocally modify the beliefs or the behaviors that are considered to be inadequate.

Before Giuliano began to scribble numbers and shapes in a meaningless, disorganized manner on the walls of his room, followed by other atypical behaviors, he was considered a model son. However, he fiercely disliked math, always preferring to draw designs and work on other creative activities. The mother and father, though, held strongly that these activities would lead nowhere and insisted that he study mathematics, so that someday he could *choose* to become an electronics engineer.

In order to develop this "hidden talent" as they called it, the parents gave him a gift for his sixteenth birthday of a very costly computer, which was never used. The father came home almost every day with a new magazine on some mathematical topic and gave it to Giuliano with much enthusiasm, but the boy left the magazines to accumulate on the shelf, without ever opening a page. The day before the crisis which led the parents to seek professional help, the mother had spent hours with her son, explaining that the basis of numbers was design and, therefore, he couldn't possibly dislike numbers.

The paradox of choice consists of requesting others to make choices that at times are well defined, as in the previous case, and at times are more or less unclear. But the request or prescription of a choice is, by its nature, totalizing and inevitably leads again to 0 learning, even when the prescribed choice is clear. Even the lower-level choice (Learning 1) contains a set of alternatives. Moreover, the choice can no longer be a choice if it is prescribed.

Still, noting that this type of paradox arose from the attempt to change others or, similarly, to influence their choice, it should be emphasized that this attempt can be acted upon with a deep conviction that the other actually has a need to change in the way that it is prescribed. In spite of this benevolent intention to bring about change and choices considered necessary—these are totalizing convictions, very common even among therapists—the final effect is to inhibit change and choices.

This type of paradox, as the others, can assume the aspect of a verbal prescription, appearing as, "You must choose for yourself" or "Do it spontaneously." More often, however, a paradoxical belief emerges from attitudes which produce behaviors that reveal attempts to change the other, even in the absence of statements such as these. The *complementary totality* that one observes most often in response to this paradox is of the type, "Please, make the choice for me." In the more serious cases (such as those defined as schizophrenic behaviors), the response can be of the type, "I choose not to choose."

This choice—the choice not to choose *is* a form of choice—allows the schizophrenic and the members of his family to develop "the art of relationship in the non-relationship, and of the non-relationship in the relationship" (Racamier, 1983, p. 34).

CHAPTER 7

❖❖❖❖❖❖❖❖❖❖❖❖❖❖❖❖❖❖❖❖❖

FROM PATHOGENIC PARADOX TO THERAPEUTIC PARADOX

"If the things that we consider misfortune and suffering, are not in reality misfortune and suffering, but only become such thanks to our own imagination, it is within our power to change them."
—Montaigne (*Complete Essays*, 1959, p. 49)

As we have seen, pathogenic paradox is initiated by some paradoxical beliefs, such as the *relationship paradox*, which produces undecidability; the *individuation paradox*, which results from an increment of dependence; the *paradox of exclusion*, which leads to the impossibility to conceptualize "both-and"; and the *paradox of choice*, which does not allow one to go beyond 0 learning.

Before we see how these limitations can be overcome through therapeutic intervention, it would be helpful to consider an aspect that is shared by both the paradoxical beliefs and by the logical and pragmatic paradoxes.

In Chapter 3, dedicated to the Recursive Chain, we have seen that paradoxes are determined by particular transgressions of the levels of complexity. Analogously, however, all other types of paradox, even paradoxical convictions, are just as much a violation of the principles of complexity, which in the circumstances described can lead to totalizing systems of relationships.

We will now examine those violations of the complexity principles and, correlatively, the premises for a psychotheraphy that takes these principles into account. These violations can be considered a specific response to the assumptions of illegitimate totality that lead to pathology.

TOLERANCE FOR AMBIGUITY

If ambiguity is a characteristic of human relationships, it is evident that it must, in some measure, be accepted by the therapist. The expectation to have a well-defined, conclusive response is the therapist's *irrational need for rationality* and his or her lack of preparedness to tolerate ambiguous messages. However, ambiguous messages, which may often appear to be irrational and incomprehensible, also have a dignity of their own. Their lack of definition is often more significant than any kind of forced definition obtained (often only temporarily) from the family or from the patient.

Symptoms in particular are, by definition, naturally endowed with ambiguity, and any attempt to reduce them to unequivocal truths are often disastrous, or unjustifiably reductive. As Haley (1986) states, "It would oversimplify an extraordinarily complex statement . . . like summarizing a Shakespearean play in a sentence" (p. 29).

The therapy must *take into account the complexity of the symptom* and respect its inherent ambiguity. The therapeutic model closest to this position is the naturalistic approach of Milton H. Erickson. According to Erickson,

> The therapist wishing to help his patient should never scorn, condemn nor reject any part of a patient's conduct simply because it is obstructive, unreasonable or even irrational. The patient's behavior is a part of the problem brought into the office: it constitutes the personal environment within which the therapy must take effect; it may constitute the dominant force in the total patient-doctor relationship. Since whatever the patient brings in to the office is in some way both a part of him and a part of his problem, the patient should be viewed with a sympathetic eye appraising the totality which confronts the therapist. In so doing the therapist should not limit himself to an appraisal of what is good and reasonable as offering possible foundations for therapeutic procedures. Sometimes, in fact, many more times than is realized, therapy can be firmly established on a sound basis only by the utilization of silly, absurd, irrational, and contradictory manifestations. (1965, p. 57)

COMPLEX TRUTHS

In the assumption of illegitimate totality that leads to pathology we find the search for absolute truth, for a certainty that could allow the resolution of a true-false dichotomy. The human tendency predominates to judge in either-or terms and to arrive at an unequivocal evaluation of every event that takes place within the surrounding reality.

If the main goal of a therapeutic intervention is to increase the range of available choices, then in accordance with the principles of complexity, therapy is not a matter of reducing the present uncertainty but (at least within certain limits) to increase it (Jantsch, 1980). Therefore, a statement can, at one and the same time, reveal itself to be both true and false: in this way one can never completely lie, nor be completely truthful.

Naturally, any therapy must not propose to eliminate every form of simplification in order to replace it with as much complexity. In so doing, we would find ourselves caught up in the same pretense to establish a totality based on the principle of either-or. Morin (1980) states: "Complexity is the combination of simplification and complexity" (p. 41). One aspect cannot lead us to exclude the other; both simplification by itself and complexity by itself lead, although in different ways, to an illegitimate totality.

PLANNING THE UNPREDICTABLE

The *capacity for prediction* and, moreover, the expectation that this prediction will be realized, play a part in the domain of simplification. The complexity of human relationships makes this capacity for prediction extremely contingent. By definition, a system acquires qualities (*positive emergence*) of its own which are not possessed singularly by any of the individuals who compose it; while individuals, in their turn, lose some qualities (*negative emergence*) that they would otherwise have had if they were not a part of that given system.

The emergence and the disappearance of these qualities make any kind of prediction about the behavior of the system very difficult. "Complexity," as stated by Jean-Louis Le Moigne (1985), based on Paul Valery's opinion, "is 'Essential Unpredictability.' "

The therapist who works with systems should not stop making predictions but must consider the prediction in the realm of possibility, not of absolute necessity. He or she must *include the unpredictable in the design of an intervention* because this can be helpful in disenchanting families from their own totalizing predictions; *and* it is desirable for therapeutic outcomes. In fact, once the obstacles that limit the family members' possible choices are removed, it is more valuable if a great number of new alternatives beyond the therapist's influence are available.

PRINCIPLES OF PARADOXICAL THERAPY

Keeping in mind these premises and the illegitimate totality that we intend to resolve, we can now examine some principles which we believe should guide one in using paradoxical therapy.

Therapy As Partiality

If the pathology is tied to an assumption of illegitimate totality, it is on this aspect that the therapy must intervene; it is this knot of undecidability that must be untied so that the system can proceed again along its life cycle. The therapist needs to remember that it is not his or her task to act upon any other areas of behavior, nor to point out any particular choice to the family.

As indicated in the preceding chapter, an illegitimate totality is fed by the presence of other convergent or divergent totalities: it tends to extinguish in the presence of nontotalizing attitudes. While in the assumption of illegitimate totality, every possible behavior is requested or prescribed. However, in paradoxical therapy requests or prescriptions are directed only toward dysfunctional behaviors. Paradoxical therapy is, therefore, a *deduction of legitimate partiality*. In fact, the therapist acts *only on one part* of the family's behaviors and/or interactive patterns, and his or her intervention is legitimized *by the request* received or by the symptom that is presented.

Paradoxical therapy is based on the principle that the therapist has a function that is limited to the resolution of illegitimate totality and related dysfunctional behaviors. The therapist does not act on other areas when he or she does not receive an explicit request to do so. The therapy is *deduced* by the same interactive patterns that the family or the patient presents. In other words, the family and/or the patient will indicate the treatment needed. The illegitimate totality or the presented symptom contains the key to the therapeutic intervention and, carried through to extreme consequences, it will ultimately resolve itself. Even from this point of view, the role of the therapist appears to be very limited. Drawing again on the thought of Erickson:

> Too many hypnotherapists take you out to dinner and then tell you what to order. I take a patient out to a psychotherapeutic dinner and I say, "You give your order." The patient makes his own selection of the food he wants. He is not hindered by my instructions, which would only obstruct and confuse his inner processes. (1980, p. 148)

The Importance of Dependence

The request or the demand for independence (individuation paradox) constitutes a crucial element of pathogenic paradox. Statements such as: "You must be independent," "Be autonomous," "Be spontaneous," "You must not listen to me," and "You must take initiatives" represent some of the more commonly known forms of this type of paradox. Naturally, as previously ascertained, it is not wholly necessary that a paradox of independence be expressed continuously through verbalizations of this type of injunction. These attitudes can also be transmitted through proposed expectations in a less explicit form: "I would like to see you settled," "At your age I knew how to live on my own," "Your sisters are already living away from home," and so on. Even simple nonverbal messages can be considered as powerful cues, for example, sighs, glances, gestures, and body postures used to comment on certain issues which signify that the issue of dependence is not yet resolved, gestures of dissent preceding attitudes of defeat, and so forth. It is also not uncommon to find behaviors analogous to those described above in some therapists when they encourage their families or their patients to assume a great degree of independence or autonomy.

In paradoxical therapy, the therapist does not encourage independence or autonomy, not because he or she does not consider this an important issue, but because this development will follow but not be contingent upon the therapeutic intervention. It is something that the family and the patient will achieve by their own means, not because it was suggested by the therapist.

Paradoxical intervention requires the *maintenance of or an increase in dependence on* the bonds in effect at the time. This must not be considered purely instrumental, as some maintain. On the contrary, it is based on the recognition of a real necessity for the bonds of dependence, of the different developmental stages of the individual, and of the individual's relationships with others.

Paradoxical therapeutic prescriptions (with respect to pathogenic paradox, which is one of the most important and least recognized distinctions) suggest, "You must be dependent," "You must not be autonomous," "You must not assume the initiative," and so on. The limitations, the bonds (and, therefore, the symptoms) are effectively considered essential for their own resolution.

Interestingly, the therapeutic paradox reintroduces the concept of time, which had vanished in the cloud of undecidability when the pathological paradox took over. Later, when the therapeutic intervention resolves these bonds, recognizing their importance, the family members can again proceed toward reciprocal individuation.

The Necessity of "Vel-vel"

At the present time, positions of the either-or type are usually less common in family therapy. In traditional family therapy, the therapist would impose alternatives upon the family such as: "Either everyone must come, or I will not do therapy," or "You must not communicate with me about the therapy outside of the session, or I will be forced to reveal what you say to all the other family members." Extreme positions of this type are now little used, and therapists realize that rigid attitudes like these are seldom justified in therapy. Nevertheless, it would be just as rigid to inexorably abandon every possible form of either-or. It is not a question of eliminating either-or, but of adding both-and.

The answer is given by the latin disjunction "vel-vel." This is a type of disjunction that does not carry mutual exclusion and includes both "both-and" and "either-or." An inclusive disjunction of this type does not exist in our language. In order to describe it, therefore, it becomes necessary to resort to the expression, vel-vel, which contains both of the other types of disjunctions. Vel-vel is, therefore, a complex disjunction composed of two simple disjunctions used conjunctively.

Since therapeutic paradox does not contain an illegitimate totality, it does not impose a simple and peremptory either-or. On the contrary, thanks to its complexity, it is in a position to provide, by means of the vel-vel, both the possibility of either-or and that of both-and. Paradoxical therapeutic intervention is not (for the one who receives it and for the one who effects it) an intervention that changes *or* maintains, or an intervention that changes *and* maintains; it is both of these possibilities, even if at different levels.

Confirmation of Choices

We have seen how the request for choices can exercise a totalizing effect. When this request meets another complementary totalization, as in the example, "Please choose for me," one develops a relationship that actually inhibits new choices. Consequently, a vicious circle (or, if you prefer, a stalemate) can develop that makes the choices extremely limited.

Nevertheless, even in severe degrees of pathology and in the most binding relationships, a choice is still possible and, actually, even impossible to eliminate. One cannot *not* choose. One can at the most *choose not to choose*, but this is still always a choice. Indeed, the choice to not choose, despite the fact that we may consider it extreme, must also be considered the higher level choice: humans are the only beings capable of the choice not to choose. Neither animals nor computers, especially, are capable of making such a choice.

Many of the problems that a therapist is called to resolve are presented in a form so repetitive and redundant that, together, they make choice impossible. A girl with a washing compulsion cannot make herself wash less; an enuretic youth cannot avoid wetting the bed; a man is not able to think of the future instead of tormenting himself with the past, and so on. These behaviors always appear to be without possible alternatives and, therefore, *seem* to be the product of an impossibility to choose. But if the person who acts in a symptomatic manner does not have the possibility to make different choices, then why or how would we ask him or her to change?

Actually, we know now that even the most serious problems are influenced by the context in which they exist: one can modify behaviors, perceptions, and so on when the circumstances in which they take place change. The girl *can* succeed in controlling her compulsive washing when she has a guest in her home; the youth does *not* always wet the bed when he sleeps at his grandparents' home; the man *is* in a position to overcome his past to help a daughter suffering through a divorce. These are only a few of the many examples that, together with the therapeutic experience of unexpected change in symptoms that seemed unchangeable, demonstrate how the possibility to effect different choices always remains consistent.

This is not to say that alternatives to the symptomatic or dysfunctional behaviors are easy for a patient or a family to correct, or that these types of behaviors are adopted only to aggravate or to make life difficult for another person. To an outside observer, the symptom (or the illegitimate totality) can appear to be the product of an impossibility to choose or a wrong choice. Actually, it simply represents the less undesirable behavior in that given moment, in that given context, and in the present level of awareness of the person acting it out.

In paradoxical therapy, the choices of the individual and of the family usually come to be *confirmed* by the therapist. There are exceptions which we shall see. *Confirmation* is an interactive pattern that has notable importance in the individual's development and to his or her relationships with others. Through means of confirmation the actions of the others receive attention; the actions are validated, and the importance of the actions is recognized. This is not to say that they must necessarily be shared: "I have watched your situation very closely and understand how important this symptom is to you now, but I cannot say that I would behave in the same way nor that you will still have this need in the future."

The confirmation of the choice by the family and by the identified patient is not, as many maintain, the product of a strategy that deceives the patient, even when the goal is to help. Rather, it is a sincere recognition of the validity of individual choices made with the tools which, at that moment, were at his or her disposal.

PARADOXICAL, PATHOGENIC, AND THERAPEUTIC RELATIONSHIPS

We have already examined some of the differences between pathogenic paradox and therapeutic paradox with regard to the respective formal characteristics, the premises, and the principles. Now we will see another important aspect which is often discussed in the literature: the difference between paradoxical pathogenic and therapeutic interactive patterns.

In "Toward a Theory of Schizophrenia," the Bateson group (Sluzki & Ransom, 1976) differentiated the pathogenic from the therapeutic double bind in this way:

The difference between the therapeutic bind and the original double bind situation is in part the fact that the therapist is not involved in a life and death struggle himself. He can therefore set up relatively benevolent binds and gradually aid the patient in his emancipation from them. (p. 22)

In this first formulation, the different aspects seem to be, above all, the noninvolvement of the therapist in a life and death struggle and of his or her "relative benevolence." But, as was followed up by Jay Haley (1963) while confirming the importance of noninvolvement, it was noted that a benevolent attitude can just as readily be taken by the family as by the therapist. He indicates that the difference is in the fact that the therapist accepts and rewards the change that follows his intervention:

The family therapist may be approaching the family in terms of "like cures like," but the outcome is different, particularly in terms of the paradoxes posed. Family members can benevolently provide an ordeal for one another, thereby imposing a paradox, but if the victim attempts to escape from the impossible situation, he is condemned for being unwilling to accept the benevolence. The therapist will provide a benevolent ordeal, but when it becomes intolerable and the family changes, the therapist accepts and rewards the change. The detachment of the therapist from the system, which is as necessary as his participation in it,

gives him a position where he can function as
a temporary intruder in the system and not a
permanent element caught up in the resistance
to change. (Haley, 1963, p. 178)

Watzlawick, Beavin, and Jackson (1967) have defined
therapeutic paradox as, structurally, "the mirror image
of a pathogenic one" (p. 241). The authors emphasized
the importance of an intense relationship; of injunctions
that create a paradox because the patient was told to
change by remaining unchanged; and of a therapeutic
situation that prevents the patient from withdrawing, or
from dissolving the paradox, by commenting on it.

Erickson, Rossi, and Rossi (1976) found the difference
between pathogenic and therapeutic paradox to be in
the positive rapport that characterizes the therapeutic
relationship, in comparison with the condition of entrapment in the family relationships where the victim of
pathogenic paradox was found; in the wide range of
therapeutic interventions, as compared to the repeated
experience of exposure to the same pathogenic double
bind; in the presence of positive injunctions instead of
negative; and in the possibility to leave the field if the
patient or family wishes to do so when rejecting a therapeutic task through which the dysfunctional behavior
develops.

Weeks and L'Abate (1982) delineate the difference
between a pathogenic and a therapeutic double bind:

A pathogenic double-bind places a person in a no-
win predicament, while a therapeutic double-
bind forces a client into a no-lose situation. In
the therapeutic double-bind there is also some

kind of intense relationship over a period of time. Within the context of therapy, the behavior the client wants to change or eliminate is prescribed or encouraged by the therapist, and the therapist implies that this reinforcement is the means of change. The client is placed in the double-bind of being told to change by staying the same. (p. 6)

Furthermore, according to these authors, in therapeutic paradox, just as in pathology, it is not permitted for the client to make the paradox dissolve by commenting on it.

Clearly emerging from these authors' various descriptions and applications of therapeutic paradox is the importance of the therapeutic relationship. It is within this context that we find the greatest difference between pathogenic and therapeutic paradox. It has become further evident that in order to be therapeutic, the paradox itself *should* be a part of a *significant but at the same time limited relationship.* An overinvolvement of the therapist could make the therapeutic paradox appear dangerously similar to the pathogenic.

One natural limitation of the therapeutic relationship is given by time factors. The ultimate goal of therapy is its conclusion; therefore, the family's relationship with the therapist is destined to be of a limited duration.

In our opinion, however, in order to avoid a totalized outcome, the therapeutic relationship should contain additional limitations. First, a therapeutic paradox *must not repeat itself,* and it must not remain unchanged over time. It must, instead, change in relation to the response that it obtains from the patient and/or from the family. Therapeutic prescriptions have a very precise and limited function and tend to extinguish themselves in a rather short time. *The area in which the therapeutic paradox intervenes is delimited*; it cannot intervene on every possible behavior (as the pathogenic paradox attempts to do) but, specifically, only on the areas of symptomatic and dysfunctional behaviors.

The *objectives* of paradoxical intervention have a second necessary limitation; the therapist must not intend to change the patient's view of the world nor to change point for point every single interactive model of the family. He or she should not intend to lead the patient in a new direction nor suggest a specific path to follow. The therapist who uses paradox wants only to resolve the undecidability in which the family and patient are caught and does not intend to interfere with and influence the decisions that the family, or patient, will later make by themselves.

It is important to note another significant aspect of the therapeutic paradoxical relationship: while in the pathogenic paradoxical relationship *attempts are made to change the other*, the therapist who uses paradox not only does not request changes in the other but also must be *available to change him or herself*. We will analyze this point more extensively later.

Therapeutic Paradox Efficacy and the Role of the "Victim"

Before summarizing the differences between pathogenic and therapeutic paradox (see Table 3), we want to briefly discuss the view, taken by many authors, that any comments about paradox on the part of the receiver of pathogenic (or therapeutic) paradox can eliminate its effectiveness. This belief derives from the time when paradox was considered to be the product of the participation of one or more persecutors toward a victim. To explain what appeared to be an incapacity on the part of the victim to defend him or herself, it was hypothesized that an injunction would prevent any comment (therefore, any undesired effect) about paradox. Now that we know there are neither victims nor persecutors, we can say that this type of injunction no longer exists, just as the impossibility to leave the field (at least after a certain age) does not exist. The identified patient, as is now recognized, participates in determining the pathogenic paradox to no less a degree than the other members of the family. In our experience, we have often observed young schizophrenics accurately comment about the presence of paradoxical injunctions or illegitimate totalities. Yet, they remained unable to extricate themselves from the paradoxical situation.

It is also not true that if the family knows that a therapeutic intervention is of the paradoxical type, its effectiveness is inhibited. Patients and families who have read books and articles about this subject and were able to comment about it to say, "This is a paradox," benefitted just as much as those who were completely unaware of the existence of paradoxical therapy. *The difference, if any, is in the therapist.* When he or she considers the paradox to be a trick that must be kept secret, it is not surprising that a therapist would be embarrassed when confronted by a family member who has discovered his or her "manipulations." Nothing of the kind can occur if the therapist is truly convinced of the validity of the paradoxical intervention applied, if the therapist presents it coher-

ently, and it is congruent with his or her own way of
thinking. If we believe that the purpose of paradox is
not to thrust the patient in the opposite direction to that
presented by the paradoxical intervention, but only to
free the individuals in the family from their undesired
bind, then the necessity for the nature of the intervention to be kept hidden will not arise.

TABLE 3
Differences Between Pathogenic Paradox
and Therapeutic Paradox

PATHOGENIC PARADOX	THERAPEUTIC COUNTERPARADOX
Recursive chain that leads to the reflexive chain	Recursive chain that leads to the stochastic process
Systematic ambiguity	Simple ambiguity
Complex contradiction	Simple contradiction
Self-reference	Stochastic process
Reflexivity	Recursive new order
Vicious circle	Absence of vicious circle
Undecidability	Decidability
Eliminates time and space	Restores time and space
No new information generated	Generates new information
Levels of learning: No access to higher levels	Levels of learning: Passage to higher levels
Assumption of illegitimate totality	Deduction of legitimate partiality
PREMISES	PRESUPPOSITIONS
Ambiguity	Tolerance of ambiguity

Continued

Search for unequivocal truth	Complex truths
Capacity of prediction	Planning the unpredictable

BELIEFS	**PRINCIPLES**
Totalization	Therapy as partiality
Paradox of individuation	Request for dependence
Paradox of exclusion	Necessity of the vel-vel
Paradox of choice	Confirmation of choice

PARADOXICAL PATHOGENIC RELATIONSHIP	**PARADOXICAL THERAPEUTIC RELATIONSHIP**
Meaningful and involving	Significant but not too involving
Totalizing	Limited
Repetitive and stereotyped interaction	Changes in interactions according to the response
Absent or reduced limits:	Notable, clear delimitation:
Notable duration	Limited duration
Involves entire relationship	Only dysfunctional areas
Objective: Change the premises	Objective: Resolve the undecidability
Tendency to change the other	Confirmation of the other's behavior
No availability for personal change	Availability of the therapist for change

IS THERAPEUTIC PARADOX A TRUE
PARADOX?

Having made the proper distinctions between therapeutic and pathogenic paradox, it is legitimate to ask
ourselves if therapeutic paradox can reasonably be defined as a true paradox. We have already described what
can be considered a true paradox and how it can develop
when the recursive chain (ambiguity, contradiction)
moves into the reflexive chain (self-reference, reflexivity, vicious circle, and undecidability).

Therapeutic and pathogenic paradox both share the
first part of this journey through the recursive chain
(and, therefore, ambiguity and contradiction). When we
reach this point, a therapeutic paradox does not merge
into the reflexive chain. As we now know, by means of a
stochastic process it generates new learning and, therefore
allows the passage to a new recursive order. In effect,
while pathogenic paradox enters a repetitive cycle that
always returns to the point of departure and, therefore,
does not produce any additional information, therapeutic paradox becomes a way to acquire new information and to access higher levels of learning.

In reality, even therapeutic paradox, to some degree,
has a repetitive modality: the recursive circuit that leads
to new learnings maintains the very same formal aspect.
This may have generated the confusion between the two
types of paradox that is sometimes experienced. However, a therapeutic paradox never returns to the point
of departure, and each time it achieves a new recursive
order. One can learn in the same way, but one always
learns different things.

From these two different premises come diametrically opposite consequences, both from the logical and pragmatic points of view. It is, therefore, a substantial difference. Actually, since the vicious circle and the undecidability do not occur, one *cannot identify the therapeutic paradox as a true paradox.*

Neither do we consider it appropriate to share the position of those who label as paradox everything that appears strange or unusual. The adjective "paradoxical," as it is commonly used to describe events of this nature, has created this confusion. However, paradox *is not the opposite of orthodox*; the opposite of orthodox is heterodox (or simply, unorthodox), as Sluzki (1987) correctly notes:

> It is useful to keep this distinction in mind because many therapeutic interventions loosely called paradoxical, are simply off-beat, unorthodox statements of therapists, which are not *para* to any prior statement or stance of the patients or their culture, and have little or no effect on the family. (p. 24)

These are the types of interventions whose effects are, for the most part, tied to surprise factors. Once recognized and brought into common use, they totally lose their efficacy. These are interventions that "do not make sense" and that have induced Paul Dell (1986) to write an article entitled "Why Do We Continue to Call Them Paradoxes?"

There is no doubt that interventions such as those previously described do not truly deserve to be called paradox. It is not because they suddenly make sense;

such interventions have always totally lacked the "logical contradiction" that is a necessary element—even if not sufficient alone—of the paradoxical structure.

Therapeutic paradoxes (for example, symptom prescription) have this character of logical contradiction. However, they lack the vicious circle of undecidability that completes a true paradox and, therefore, they cannot either, in a strict sense, be identified as paradox. Nevertheless, they are structured to partially resemble the structure of a true paradox (the pathogenic), and this is probably the reason why the therapeutic paradox demonstrates an extraordinary therapeutic specificity in dissolving the pathogenic paradox. The therapeutic paradox binds itself to the pathogenic, interrupting the circuit that leads to the reflexive chain and, instead, leads again to the recursive evolution that seemingly had become inaccessible.

This specificity of effect between pathogenic paradox and therapeutic paradox resembles that of antibodies that respond only to the antigen that has stimulated their production. In order to be effective, it must be perfectly calibrated for the dysfunctional area on which it must intervene, and in the absence of an illegitimate totality, this intervention shows itself to be totally inadequate.

Given these peculiar features, it would be more appropriate to call this type of therapeutic intervention not paradox, but *counterparadox*, as was first done by Mara Selvini Palazzoli and colleagues (1975). From now on we will utilize the term counterparadox or refer to it, even if we use the term therapeutic paradox at times for practical purposes. Therapeutic paradox is a term that, although largely unjustified, has been legitimized by current common use.

CHAPTER 8

❖❖❖❖❖❖❖❖❖❖❖❖❖❖❖❖❖❖❖❖❖❖

THERAPEUTIC COUNTERPARADOX

CLASSIFICATIONS OF COUNTERPARADOXICAL INTERVENTIONS

Many different classifications regarding counterparadoxical interventions currently exist. Haley (1963) and more recently Seltzer (1986) examine paradox from the perspective of the different approaches in which it is utilized. The extensive and noted work of Weeks and L'Abate (1982) offers yet another review that distinguishes paradoxes on the basis of level (individual, interactional, systemic) at which they act or, as in the study of Rohrbaugh, Tennen, Press, and White (1981), on a compliance/defiance model. We propose a view based on the structure of counterparadox; we maintain that while counterparadoxical interventions are established on the same principles, they differ most in their formal aspects.

Essentially, a therapeutic counterparadox (as intended in this work) is defined as *an intervention of confirmation of the symptom and other dysfunctional behaviors that*

TABLE 4
Counterparadoxical Interventions

COUNTERPARADOXICAL DEFINITIONS	COUNTERPARADOXICAL INJUNCTIONS
Positive definitions Positive connotation Reframing Relabeling Deemphasizing the symptom Reversal Ascribing noble intentions *Negative definitions* Restraint techniques Declaration of impotence Impotence tactics Pathological or negative redefintion Confusional redefinition	Paradoxical intention Prescribing the symptom Scheduling the symptom Prescribing rituals Rules prescription Prescribing elements of the symptom complex Splitting Positioning Paradoxical ordeal Provocative therapy Pretending Benign sabotage Encouraging resistance Metaphoric tasks Advertising instead of concealing Paradoxical letters Giving in to the symptom Prescription to "Go Slow" Inhibiting and prohibiting change Relapse prescription Prescription of multiple alternatives

COUNTERPARADOXICAL PREDICTIONS
Relapse prediction Predicting the negative consequences of change

do not require change—if at all, in a very limited form—of the habitual patterns aimed at resolving undecidability, without pointing out possible later choices.

Our classification of paradoxes is simple; it takes into account the analogies that can be drawn between therapeutic counterparadox and a true paradox. In fact, we have:

- Counterparadoxical *definitions*;
- Counterparadoxical *injunctions*; and
- Counterparadoxical *predictions*.

Definitions, injunctions, and predictions correspond to the diverse forms that a paradoxical, logical, and/or pragmatic structure can assume. From the pragmatic point of view, these three diverse forms are actually interchangeable: this cannot occur in the sphere of logic.

Within the framework of human relationships, a paradoxical definition always implies an injunction and a prediction, in the same way that an injunction always implies a definition and a prediction, and so on. For example, a husband could say to his wife, "I am not a trustworthy person." This paradoxical definition of oneself usually leads to the undecidable vicious circle: if the wife believes his statement, she cannot trust him, if she cannot trust him, she cannot not believe his statement and therefore she trusts him.* It also carries the paradoxical injunction, "You must not trust me" and the paradoxical prediction, "No one will ever trust me."

---

*In reality this totalization by the husband tends to generate undecidability, but it will only occur if it is enforced by a corresponding totalizing attitude of the wife when confronting his statement.

Actually, if the wife simply attributes limited and contingent values to the statement and considers it not solidly connected to all past, present, and future behaviors of the husband, she would be able to maintain her trust in him and to simply not believe his statement without extending it to the entire relationship.

This pragmatic effect of any paradoxical proposition also occurs in the case of counterparadoxical therapy. The positive connotation of a symptom (counterparadoxical definition) always has the effect of a prescriptive (injunction and prediction) type. For example, to reframe the symptomatic behavior of an agoraphobic patient as "a legitimate necessity to remain in the house in order to learn about herself without being distracted by the presence of others" is equivalent to an injunction not to go out. If she attempts to venture outside of the house it may be considered a prediction of a worsening behavior.

Given the correspondence of various forms of paradox, the choice of one or the other under different circumstances is dictated, as will be seen, by specific cues. The value of this classification is not, therefore, exclusively theoretical.

Counterparadoxical Definitions

In logic, paradoxical *definitions* are also called semantic antinomy, and certainly the most famous is that of the liar. In psychotherapy, different aspects of the family system can be defined by the therapist in a counterparadoxical form. Among the most noted counterparadoxical definitions are the following:

Positive Connotation (Selvini Palazzoli et al., 1975) defines, positively, the *homeostatic tendency* of the system.

Reframing (Watzlawick, Weakland, & Fisch, 1974) redefines the *context* or the frame of reference.

Relabeling (Haley, 1963; Grunebaum & Chasin, 1978) *changes the definitions of the symptomatic behavior.*

Deemphasizing the Symptom (Minuchin, 1974) redefines the *severity* of the symptom.

Reversal (Bowen, 1972) offers a definition that represents the dysfunctional behaviors in a way that *contrasts with habitual patterns.*

Ascribing Noble Intentions (Stanton, 1981) redefines the *intentions* of the family members.

All of these counterparadoxical definitions (it would be more correct to speak of redefinitions since they modify definitions that were given previously) attribute a positive value to the symptom or show it in a positive frame. But it should be emphasized that every positive redefinition of the symptom, or of the dysfunctional behaviors, carries with it a negative redefinition of the possible change.

There are, in fact, negative definitions of behavior that implicitly define the symptom as obviously positive. These are *Restraint Techniques* (Watzlawick et al., 1974), through which *change becomes redefined as undesirable or disadvantageous*; *Declaration of Impotence* (Selvini Palazzoli et al., 1975); and *Impotence Tactics* (Whitaker, 1977). The latter two definitions have an analogous function in which the therapist admits he or she can no longer conduct the therapy. In this way the therapist defines him- or herself as impotent, but at the same time redefines the impotence of the family facing the symptom as pos-

itive and *the impulse to change* as negative. Whitaker
(1977) states:

> One of the things that I think is important in
> facing my impotence is that the reason they [the
> families] come is because they are facing *their*
> impotence, and that is a very humiliating thing.
> It has been hard for them to reach this point
> —to accept that they are impotent, that they
> aren't making it, and that their win-lose score
> for last season was so bad they are going to have
> to change coaches or hire a new one. I think
> of families as having one universal symptom,
> and that symptom is the impulse to change.
> (p. 70)

Redefinition in general and counterparadoxical redefinition in particular have much importance in therapy. They allow one to present preexisting relationships
in a new light, in a different view. In dysfunctional families, the capacity to redefine is markedly reduced, while
it is certainly one of the most important premises in
order for a relationship to evolve.

Each of the various phases of the life cycle is marked
by as many processes of redefinition of one's individual
interactive patterns and of their rules. If redefinition
does not take place, the passage to the next phase of the
life cycle becomes blocked.

For example, the "weaning process" of children by
the parents does not consist of only a reciprocal physical
separation; it is, instead, a complex redefinition of the
interactive patterns in the entire system. A physical separation, without negotiating new interactive rules in the

system, is not at all indicative of the completion of an effective process of individuation. However, if a redefinition of the interactive rules is realized, there can be a true individuation even without physical departure. This explains the importance of redefinition in therapy, to the family and to the therapist, as a form of training to acquire the flexibility necessary for the continuous evolution of systems in transformation.

The redefinition most often used in therapy is certainly that which attributes positive value to the dysfunctional behaviors and negative value to change. Nevertheless, in our experience, we have to note that cases do exist in which it is more appropriate to facilitate the opposite. In one very interesting study, Grunebaum and Chasin (1978) used *pathological or negative relabeling*, thereby worsening the diagnoses of their patients. The outcome was an improvement in the family relationships and in the patient's behavior.

From our experience we maintain that *Pathological or Negative Redefinition* is particularly indicated with families in which parents have relinquished their roles and, consequently, are undermined by the children. It is also indicated with families of depressed patients, as in the following case:

> Ileana is again on the verge of a serious and painful depression, the natural consequence, for her, of a lifetime of mistakes and wrongs that she feels she has committed to others throughout the years. Her marriage is now in crisis. She admits that some of the problems depend on her husband's behavior. Nevertheless, she believes she is really to blame: she

doesn't know how to take him; he would probably be completely different if he had married
another woman, and so on. Her only son, 15
years old, suffers from bronchial asthma, and
Ileana feels responsible because she worked
when he was a baby and, therefore, probably
neglected him.

The woman also blames herself for her parents' distress; she married without their approval. She also feels guilty for having caused,
directly or indirectly, her sisters' suffering. The
eldest sister married a friend of Ileana's husband, who betrayed her, and she subsequently
developed a very serious form of obesity; the
younger sister was jilted by another friend of the
husband's to whom Ileana had introduced her.
Ileana remains convinced that she has "ruined"
her sisters' lives.

During the session, the therapist said he believed that Ileana did not reveal everything and
that there was underlying guilt which went
much deeper than what she had admitted. Even
more surprising for him, he remarked, was the
fact that the family members had tolerated this
assumption of guilt for everyone and everything.

The entire family was shocked by the therapist's comments: for years everyone thought
that Ileana had burdened herself with non-
existent guilt. The remarks that the therapist
directed to Ileana, therefore, seemed to them
incomprehensible. In the past, they all tried to
convince her that she had no reason to feel

guilty, while now, they were being repri-
manded by the therapist for having been her
accomplices. In addition, until now, they had
not thought that they could possibly be angry
with a person who blamed herself for wrongs
that, in their opinion, she had not even committed.

The therapist made it clear that Ileana is
guilty of a serious presumption which led her
to feel responsible for everyone and everything
she encountered. She believed herself able to
create happiness and/or unhappiness for all the
others.

The family members seemed relieved, finally. Now they knew they could (or better yet,
they must, if they did not want to be her accomplices) treat her as any other human being.

Most likely, whether Ileana mentions her
guilt during the remainder of her therapy depends on the different family attitudes toward
her. Ileana no longer represents the entire system. "The guilt for feeling guilty" was her way
of seeing herself, which the family accepted and
colluded in. Now that totalizing belief is less
acceptable, even for her.

This case indicates that it is not as important to express
appreciation through a positive redefinition to the patient and/or to the family as it is to confirm the family's
experience, their interactional modes, and their world
view, however dysfunctional and unsatisfactory they
seem. Therefore, redefinition does not necessarily have
to be positive. When the family and the patient have a

negative view of themselves and of the needs of the others, it is often more helpful to apply a negative redefinition.

The therapist must express approval or disapproval only when he or she really approves or disapproves. Otherwise, the therapist does no more than offer the family a chain of compliments that he does not himself believe. In our opinion, the use of therapeutic paradoxes based on pretense—a positive view of the family and of the designated patient with the only goal being to please them in order to obtain their cooperation—must be considered the most frequent cause of failure in paradoxical therapy.

If the therapist does not believe in a positive redefinition, it is preferable that he or she does one of the following things:

1. Search among the many possible aspects of a symptomatic behavior for another positive aspect about which he or she is more strongly convinced.
2. Consider the possibility of using a negative redefinition that he or she is disposed to believe, if it corresponds with a real need to be devalued, which constitutes the totalizing belief of the family, for example, "We are always wrong in everything."
3. Abstain from using redefinitions.

All too often in systemic therapy interventions are planned and implemented that take into account only the family's beliefs and not the therapist's. A therapist who does not believe in what he or she says and/or does will end up devaluing the intervention. Sooner or later, the family cannot help but realize they have been deceived or misled.

CONFUSIONAL REDEFINITION.

This is yet another way to redefine family system interactions. It is indicated for families with a high level of confusion and also indicated for therapists who do not have a clear idea of what form of redefinition to use. Confusional redefinition is a combination of two or more possibly contrasting definitions, which intentionally creates confusion. It produces a strong need to search for possible alternative definitions. This technique is a derivation of the *Confusion Technique* created by Milton Erickson (1964b):

> . . . a presentation of ideas and understandings conducive of mental activity and response, but so intermingled with seemingly related valid but actually nonpertinent communications, that responses are inhibited, frustration and uncertainty of mind engendered, and the culmination is then in a final suggestion permitting a ready and easy response satisfying to the subject and validated by the subject's own, though perhaps unrecognized by the self, experimental learnings. (pp. 183–207)

In confusional redefinition the therapist simply increases, with his definitions, the preexisting confusion without adding a suggestion, a prescription, or any other type of clarifying intervention. The possibility of reorganizing themselves, after the confounding intervention is delivered, is left to the family, as in the following case:

Lou and Barbara seem incapable of clearly defining what they want from therapy. In particular, they are uncertain about whether to remain together or to separate. At the end of every session, they cannot even decide whether or not they intend to continue therapy.

After some futile attempts to obtain a clear direction from the couple, the therapists decided to utilize a confusional redefinition that was first meticulously prepared and then presented to the couple this way:

"We have thought about your situation very carefully and have now reached a conclusion: we do not know if in your case it is better to stay together or to separate, but we know for certain that the best way for you to stay together is to be separate; while the best way for you to be separate is to stay together. We also do not know whether, if you stay together or separate, it is possible to have the courage to be separate staying together, or to have the courage to be together, staying separate; or, if you simply prefer to be separated or to stay together. We do not even know if you should be here together, because to be here with us in therapy, would be to say you are separated by us. In this case, it would probably be better to have therapy separate by us and, therefore, in a certain sense to be together."

After having listened to this tortuous discourse, the couple remained for a few minutes in absolute silence. They seemed to be immersed in deep reflection, but the contents of these thoughts were never revealed to the therapists. Soon after, the husband, with unusual determination, asked to make another appointment.

When they returned two weeks later, the therapists became aware that the wife had left home unexpectedly following the last session and did not tell her husband where she was going. She stayed with her sister who lived in the next building where she was able to watch her husband from a window. After a week of searching, the husband finally succeeded in tracking her down—only a few steps from home. From this experience, both arrived at the conclusion that they could not stay apart, and they decided to remain together. At this point, however, they asked if they should discontinue therapy. The response given was that the best way to stay with the therapists is to stay away from them. By then, they had maintained this "distant-closeness" from therapy.

Counterparadoxical Injunctions

Injunctions consist of requesting certain determined behaviors of another person. As we have seen with counterparadoxical definitions, even injunctions tend to emphasize the importance of the symptom and the undesirability of change. In comparison to definitions, injunctions do not limit themselves to giving a significance to a particular behavior; instead, they prescribe it or prohibit it. Some of the most noted paradoxical injunctions are the following:

Paradoxical Intention (Frankl, 1939, 1947): The *intentional reproduction of the symptom* is prescribed. Frankl actually coined this phrase for the first time in 1947 in a book that never was translated from the German. Nevertheless, the author had previously described this technique as a method to eliminate the anticipatory anxiety that precedes the onset of the symptom.

Prescribing the Symptom (Haley, 1963; Watzlawick et al., 1967): The first, and probably the best known, of the paradoxical interventions utilized in family therapy.

Scheduling the Symptom (Newton, 1968): The request is given to the patient, the couple, or the family *to schedule the frequency, intensity, and duration of the dysfunctional behaviors*.

Prescribing Rituals (Selvini Palazzoli et al., 1975): The *repetitive ritualistic behaviors* of the family that accompany the symptom are prescribed in order to establish "new norms that tacitly substitute (replace) the previous ones" (p. 107).

Rules Prescription (Andolfi, 1977): The family system is requested to reproduce their own *dysfunctional rules*.

Prescribing Elements of the Symptom Complex (Zeig, 1980): In direct or indirect form the therapist prescribes not the symptom itself, but some of its *components*, among which Zeig indicates the cognitive, the affective, the behavioral, the contextual, the relational, the attitudinal, and the symbolic.

Splitting (Lankton & Lankton, 1986): The *symptom is broken up* into a series of consecutive passages, of which only the first is prescribed, in a way that makes it no longer necessary to arrive at the final consequences of the symptom.

Positioning (Rohrbaugh et al., 1981): The position of the patient is accepted and exaggerated, in the sense that all the implications of the behavior that the patient has not previously taken into account are evaluated and prescribed.

Paradoxical Ordeal (Haley, 1973, 1984; Madanes, 1984): The symptomatic behavior is prescribed, but with some unpleasant quality added.

Provocative Therapy (Farrelly & Brandsma, 1974): *Provocatory prescriptions of the symptom* are used often, with the goal of stimulating the patient's and the family's reaction.

Pretending (Madanes, 1980, 1984): Pretending can assume diverse forms such as asking for, usually through the parents, *the symbolic representation of the symptom*; asking for the *deliberate reproduction of the symptom's function*; asking to *upset the hierarchical relationship*.

Benign Sabotage (Watzlawick et al., 1974): This consists of prescribing *incongruent symptoms or behaviors to the parents in order to sabotage the rebellious attitudes* or insubordination of the children.

Encouraging Resistance (Erickson, 1964-a; 1964a; Haley, 1973): In this case the counterparadoxical prescription regards the *resistances* that are thought to be dysfunctional to the course of therapy.

Metaphoric Tasks (Haley, 1973, 1976, Haley in de Shazer, 1980): A request is brought to the family to "enact the troublesome pattern in a modified form and in a different context. . . . When performing this sort of task, families will often spontaneously rewrite the ending of the metaphor, which in turn helps to further undermine the original, troublesome pattern upon which it is modeled" (de Shazer, p. 473).

Advertising Instead of Concealing (Watzlawick et al., 1974): The patient and/or family are asked *not to conceal* and, therefore, *to more openly produce the symptoms that cause discomfort*. This intervention is based on the principle that the solution adopted (the attempt to hide) is the problem and addresses the elimination of the anticipatory anxiety. The symptom is prescribed together with the accompanying discomfort.

Paradoxical Letters (Weeks & L'Abate, 1982): Other forms of therapeutic paradox, usually presented orally, can be utilized in writing.

Giving in to the Symptom (Watzlawick et al., 1974): Prescribes not so much the symptom, as the sense of defeat that the symptom brings.

The Prescription to "Go Slow" (Watzlawick et al., 1974; Fisch, Weakland, & Segal, 1982): *Requests that changes take place very gradually*. This prescription is usually accompanied by the justification that change which occurs slowly is usually more lasting.

Inhibiting and Prohibiting Change (Weeks & L'Abate, 1982): One is asked to *postpone or block any possible change* and/or good reasons to justify the prohibition are given.

Relapse Prescription (Haley, 1973; Weakland, Fisch, Watzlawick, & Bodin, 1974): Contains a request to bring the symptom back following its disappearance which is considered premature.

We acknowledge the impossibility of including in this work a thorough and extensive list of all counterparadoxical techniques, but we believe that those reported offer at least an idea of the great number of counterparadoxical interventions that may be utilized in family therapy. In particular, we note that prescriptive interventions are more frequently used than redefinition and predictions. Certainly family therapy has always attributed great importance to interventions of the prescriptive type. This is perhaps due to the fact that family therapy has evidenced, more than any other perspective, the prominent role played by the use of prescriptions in human relations. The systemic perspective has greatly emphasized the *ubiquitous presence of prescribing* behaviors, going so far as to state that prescriptions are unavoidable and that each single behavioral act corresponds to a prescription (Canevelli, Loriedo, Pezzi, Trasarti Sponti, & Vella, 1981).

It is evident, therefore, that the therapist cannot *not* prescribe and cannot *not* receive prescriptions. His or her work will, therefore, be above all that of selecting the prescriptive behaviors which are more suitable to the patient or family in therapy. In Chapter 9 we will discuss the criteria that one can follow in choosing the most appropriate counterparadoxical prescriptions in different situations.

Prescriptions or counterparadoxical injunctions usually consist of a request for something that is already happening, and in such a way that leaves the initiative for possible change to the individuals and to the family. Whitaker (1977) proposes a type of intervention which in appearance does not seem to be a paradox because it consists in proposing alternatives; however, the alternatives are proposed in such a way that the initiative always remains in the patient's and in the family's hands.

The *Prescription of Multiple Alternatives*, as we will call this type of intervention, consists of offering a range of possibilities—realistic or absurd, but congruent with the request received by the therapist—so wide that the therapist will be able to avoid pointing out any one as valid and, at the same time, will be able to help the family realize that there are alternatives to the present situation. An example of this is offered by Whitaker (1977) in the following case:

> I had a lady call me up and say, "I'm married to this goddam doctor and I've got five kids, and the only thing that is going to work is to divorce him." I say, "Well, what do you want from me?" She said, "I think that we ought to have an interview first." "Okay," say I, "bring him along." So she arrived and started the same line again about her only option being a divorce. I say, "You know, that's crazy. There are many other options. You can shoot the son-of-a-bitch, you can ruin his reputation in town by inferring that he is a homosexual or . . . you can take off with all his money and go to San Francisco. There are all sorts of possibilities and I think that you should consider all of them and not just the one you mentioned. I have several others but they don't come to mind at the moment." (p. 73)

Counterparadoxical Predictions

According to Watzlawick (1965), paradoxical *predictions* "derive their power, charm and importance from the fact that they can arise only within the context of an *ongoing interaction* between people" (p. 369). Nevertheless, the pragmatic quality that characterizes this type of paradox and the effects of paradoxical predictions on human relationships have been little studied.

In their logical structure, paradoxical predictions are based on the anticipation of an unforeseen event. In this case, the illegitimate totalization is in the fact that included among all predictable events are those which are unpredictable. Beginning with this idea, we soon arrive at an undecidable vicious circle in which an event is predictable only if it is unpredictable, or it is unpredictable only if it is predictable.

Counterparadoxical predictions are based on this same principle. They are usually established by means of the prediction of an event that, by itself, takes place in the category of the unpredictable: the occurrence and change of the symptom with all the consequences that it generates. Two well-noted counterparadoxical predictions are the following:

Relapse Prediction (Haley, 1973): Usually this type of intervention is acted upon when the premature disappearance of a symptomatic behavior gives reason to expect a relapse.

Predicting the Negative Consequences of Change: The prediction of a relapse, or of a worsening, has the same effect as a prescription of the symptom but with a future projection. It can even be put into effect by reporting the possible negative consequences that could arise before the change occurs.

If the symptom has not totally vanished, but has simply improved, one can predict a worsening.

Definitions, injunctions, and counterparadoxical predictions (formally, they are no more than different modalities of counterparadoxical interventions) tend to overlap because they *correspond to only one therapeutic principle and to one common goal.* In addition, there also exist complex interventions in which different forms of counterparadox can be used simultaneously. Similarities and differences between the various forms of interventions have a fundamental value in the choice of the most appropriate therapeutic counterparadox.

CHAPTER 9

◈◈◈◈◈◈◈◈◈◈◈◈◈◈◈◈◈◈◈◈◈◈◈

CONSTRUCTING PARADOXICAL INTERVENTIONS

THE USE OF CONFIRMATION AS THE BASIC STRUCTURE OF COUNTERPARADOXICAL INTERVENTIONS

As demonstrated in the preceding chapter, the classification of the different therapeutic paradoxes in definitions, injunctions, and predictions based on the formal aspects of counterparadox does not have a purely theoretical value, being that these are used in the construction of the proper paradoxical therapeutic intervention. Classifying therapeutic paradoxes in this way proves to be very useful in selecting the paradox most appropriate for each individual situation.

The modality of selection and construction of paradoxical interventions that we present is modeled on the pattern of "confirmation," which we consider to be of fundamental importance in the application of therapeutic paradox. *Confirmation involves observing, recogniz-*

ing, respecting, and validating the ongoing interactive behaviors, including, above all, those behaviors which are symptomatic and dysfunctional. Confirmation, therefore, has no absolute value in that it is directed at present behaviors only and, thus, cannot always be constant. Instead, it must be modified over time in relation to any changes in the symptomatic and dysfunctional behaviors.

The confirmation of symptomatic behaviors is *not* based on the idea that using any type of strategy is legitimate in trying to to eliminate a symptom, as is often the case with many therapists who use paradox. The premises on which the confirmation is based are notably different:

1. The genuine *respect* on the part of the therapist for the ongoing interactive patterns in the family;
2. The *recognition of the potentialities* that are inherent even in the most regressive behaviors; and
3. The *flexibility* that allows the therapist to adapt to the characteristics of each individual family system and, in particular, to their repetitive behaviors.

We must continue to stress the importance of not considering counterparadox a trick that can be built into any attempted strategy intended to eliminate the symptom and the importance of not adopting, throughout the course of therapy, false redefinitions, prescriptions, and paradoxical predictions. But this suggestion could run the risk of being nothing more than a useless exhortation until we make clear how it can be realized.

There are certain aspects that distinguish those therapists who correctly apply counterparadox from those who use it without believing in what they do and say. We have often observed that families can easily make this distinction. There is a certain air of distrust that accompanies, for example, a therapist's positive redefinition which is not honest. In our opinion, the therapist demonstrates his or her own authenticity in the use of therapeutic counterparadox if—in the selection, the construction, and the application of counterparadox—he or she follows three principles which are the basis of the confirmation model:

1. Observing the symptom and redundant behaviors;
2. Utilizing the symptom and repetitive behaviors; and
3. Tailoring the therapeutic intervention.

Observing the Symptom and Redundant Behaviors

Careful observation of the symptom, as well as of all redundant behaviors, renders the therapist able to make a correct diagnosis and to identify all the characteristics that allow him to select an appropriate intervention. Without accurate observation, therefore, it is not possible to apply a correct counterparadoxical intervention; one cannot confirm that which one does not see.

The care the therapist puts into observing and gathering data is also important information transmitted to the family. It can demonstrate a genuine interest by the therapist for what takes place in the family and in what he or she has observed. The therapist's competence is often a correlate of his or her ability to observe, rather

than his or her use of sophisticated techniques. Learning
to observe redundant patterns in the patient's and family's behaviors should constitute the most relevant part
in the training of a systemic therapist.

Utilizing the Symptom and Repetitive Behaviors

Erickson (1958) introduced the concept of *utilization* as
a therapeutic technique; it is also a general principle of
his therapeutic model. According to this principle, repetitive behaviors can be utilized in a therapeutic sense,
even when they are symptoms or resistance.

We consider utilization the most valid means to effect
confirmation. When a behavior is utilized, it is implicitly
redefined and prescribed. Therefore, the positive value
of the symptom is not only simply stated by the therapist,
but also demonstrated by its utilization. Moreover, if the
therapist succeeds in utilizing the symptom, the patient
and the family can also learn to utilize it.

When the symptom is utilized, it maintains its dignity
of behavior while it loses its formal characteristics (stereo-
typed repetition, incomprehensibility, involuntariness,
and tendency toward disorder). Therapeutic counterparadox proposes, in fact, to confirm the contents of
the symptom, modifying only its formal aspects.

Tailoring the Therapeutic Intervention

The principle of *tailoring* indicates the importance of
modeling the therapeutic intervention upon the characteristics of the family as they are presented in therapy,

with respect to the modality of interaction in progress. Tailoring is the consequence of observation and of utilization—when the repetitive aspects of the family are diligently observed and then utilized in an intervention calibrated to the needs of each individual family.

CONSTRUCTING COUNTERPARADOXICAL INTERVENTIONS

Counterparadoxical interventions must take the form of a precise response to the problem (or symptom) presented by the family. Since every family, in presenting the problem, shows determined characteristics, one must also take these characteristics into account in order to establish a well-suited intervention.

The Family's Interactive Style

The interactive style of the family must be known by the therapist in order for him or her to adequately select and elaborate the paradoxical intervention. For example, prescriptions presented in a vague and poorly defined form prove to be ineffective for families having a rigid and compulsive style of interaction. With this type of family, it is appropriate instead to give prescriptions with meticulous precision or in the form of a ritual. On the other hand, for families with a chaotic mode of interaction, the use of little detailed interventions, or even of confusional techniques, will certainly prove more valid than a program of rules and methodical, rigidly organized, procedures.

It is also important to identify the family themes—
those issues that occupy the major portion of the family's
conversation. These themes generally indicate areas that
have particular significance for the family. As an example, the members of the family may often speak of
food, education, and money. The therapist may at first
consider that these issues have only an incidental interest
for therapy, however, they often reveal, directly or indirectly, important associations to fundamental aspects
of the family's life.

Some families say more when they speak about the
weather than when they discuss their true underlying
conflicts. Analogously, the therapist in such a situation
most often obtains the best results by using significant
metaphors during a discussion of weather than when he
or she intervenes in their existing conflicts in a direct
manner.

The language of the family is another aspect that the
therapist cannot ignore if he or she intends to utilize
counterparadox through the confirmation model. Every
family has its own language, and in order to be understood, the therapist must be able to join the family and
speak its language. At the very least, the therapist must
modify his or her own language until it becomes understandable to the family. A classic example of not
speaking the same language might be the case of a therapist who uses extremely technical terms and concepts
with a family who uses only simple language. Some families are more sensitive to nonverbal communication. For
other families it is essential to have intense conversa-
tions. When the family presents a language in which
fantasy has a prominent role, the most appropriate form

of intervention would utilize metaphors, anecdotes, and fables.

The phrase "Your marriage is a *zero sum game*" would probably not make too much sense to the majority of couples who are in therapy. On the other hand, it can be a way of using confirmation if the couple consist of two mathematicians.

The problem presented by the family can give the therapist the greatest indications for the construction of counterparadoxical interventions. For this reason we will dedicate some time to this aspect.

The Presenting Problem

The problem presented to the therapist by the family is usually the result of a long process of selection that has taken place within the family. The problem usually encompasses many other problems, but it represents the *point of convergence of the totalities of all family members*. The problem or the symptom that the family presents is the only behavior consistent with the family's logic, even when that logic appears profoundly distorted and inadequate. The coherence between the symptomatic behavior and the logic of the family, and the correspondence which can be found between the presenting problem and the illegitimate totalities of the family, can explain how a small modification that is used to intervene in this area can result in profound changes in the family structure.

The quality and the quantity of information contained in the presenting problem or in the symptom make this limited segment of the family interactive behavior the principal instrument of therapeutic change. Observation, utilization, tailoring, and therefore, the confirmation of the problem constitute the principal framework of therapeutic counterparadox. One could paraphrase the well-known statement by Watzlawick, Weakland, and Fisch (1974, p. 82), "the solution reveals itself as the . . . problem" by reversing it to state that "the problem itself *is* the solution."

We will now consider some aspects of the presenting problem on the basis of which it is possible to construct counterparadoxical therapeutic interventions:

1. The description of the family problem;
2. The content of the problem;
3. The form of the problem; and
4. The evolution of the problem.

THE DESCRIPTION OF THE FAMILY PROBLEM

A family coming to therapy may describe the problem or the symptom as suffering that must cease, as a desire for change, as an intolerable situation, or as a need for help. The therapist can make use of the way in which the family describes the problem, utilizing it as a motivation for change. He or she can then construct the counterparadoxical intervention in such a way that it is presented to the family as a means to end the suffering, to satisfy the desire to change, to resolve an intolerable situation, or to receive help.

THE CONTENT OF THE PROBLEM

Different types of requests can be presented to the therapist by different families. The content of the request must be given careful attention by the therapist because it will hold, for him or her, many clues for selecting the most suitable type of paradox for each family. The requests that the therapist receives are most often of three types: "Why?"; "What can be done?"; and "What will happen?"

The form for the first type of request is usually presented in a question such as "Why is our child behaving this way?" This type of presentation is usually given by families who tend to wait for the therapist to give an explanation of, say, the child's symptomatic behavior. They are, therefore, predominantly oriented toward the *past* in seeking a justification to the present situation. In this case, since the family awaits an *explanation*, the type of counterparadox most appropriate will be a *paradoxical definition* of the designated patient and of his or her symptomatic behavior.

The second type of request is more or less presented in the form, "What must we do with our child when he or she behaves like this?" This type of family wishes to receive concrete and specific *directions* about what to do, and it shows a prevalent orientation toward the *present* in their search for an immediate solution to their problem. These cases, therefore, mainly indicate interventions of the *paradoxical prescriptive* type, which contain suggestions on what to do.

In the third type of request the family waits for the therapist to express his prognostic judgment on the possible *future evolution* of the presenting problem: "What will happen to our child who behaves like this?" These are families usually oriented toward the *future*, a future they look to with trepidation and worry. Cases of this kind call for an intervention of the *paradoxical prediction* type in which the therapist points out what will be, according to him or her, the possible evolution of the problem.

THE FORM OF THE PROBLEM

The problem can be presented in many different forms, which are usually connected to the family's dysfunctional behaviors. The cases to which we have so far made reference are those in which the problem or symptom is very well defined and clearly presented by the family. Consequently, with these families we can apply the principles indicated above and utilize redefinitions, prescriptions, or counterparadoxical predictions. Unfortunately, problems are not always presented clearly. We sometimes encounter families who describe the problem in an *ambiguous form*.

The ambiguous problem   This situation often occurs when the family presents more than one problem and is not able to establish a clear hierarchy of importance between them. In this situation, the therapist can find himself or herself in trouble: any effort to understand which problem should be the focus of intervention results in the inability of the family to indicate only one problem at a time. This inability may be due to disagreement between the members of the family about exactly which problem is *the* problem, or from the family's need to maintain an ambiguous definition of the problem. The therapist's efforts to obtain a clear and unequivocal definition are almost always futile. In that event, it is preferable to *accept the ambiguous form* that the family gives to the problem and to respond with a *multiple counterparadoxical intervention*.

The multiple counterparadoxical intervention contains a number of therapeutic paradoxes; thus, every problem can receive a specific response, as described in the following case:

> Rose is 16 years old and some months ago had begun to wash everything she and family members touched with soap and disinfectant. She spends her entire day tending to this activity. Her mother became worried about Rose's behavior and is afraid that this might be a serious illness; the father does not share the mother's opinion. According to him, it is the mother who is sick: she had always had an obsession about cleaning and was not aware that it was no different from what Rose was doing. According to him, the mother considers the girl sick only because she is the one person who dared to interfere with her own absurd cleaning rituals, which she imposed not only upon herself, but on the entire family.
>
> The maternal grandmother, who lived with the family from the time the parents were married, considers the father the only real problem in the family. In her opinion, the wife and daughter had been forced to be obsessed with taking care of the things in the house since he was a miser. He insisted that everything be kept like new, so he wouldn't have to buy anything. It was exactly like her husband who had died the year before.
>
> The therapist became confused by these diverse descriptions of the problem. He soon re-

alized that he could offer no one alternative to all of these ambiguous definitions of the problem. *Each* of them would have to be considered as the target of a therapeutic intervention. It was required, therefore, that each receive an appropriate redefinition in such a way that the different redefinitions would not be in opposition to each other. Rose's behavior was redefined as an attempt to help the mother who always worked too hard cleaning the house. The mother's excessive cleaning was explained as her wish to satisfy her husband by keeping everything neat, orderly, and like new. The reason for the husband not wanting to buy anything new was redefined as his wish to save his wife from having more things to clean. The mother's concern for Rose was because she didn't want her to make sacrifices as she herself had. The husband's criticism of his wife was to stop her from driving herself crazy trying to please him and, finally, the mother-in-law's criticism of the son-in-law was to make him aware of how much he reminded her of the husband she had lost.

When an ambiguous request involves two different problems, which often occurs in couples therapy, the therapist can resort to a *combined counterparadoxical intervention* that consists of utilizing both problems, combining them in such a way that one serves as a solution for the other, as in the following case:

Daniela and Claudio bitterly complained about each other. To Daniela, her husband was a man who had an extreme sense of duty, which compelled him to constantly be preoccupied with responsibilities. He spent three to four hours extra at work every day, checking and rechecking his work to be sure everything was done perfectly. In spite of this, he is never satisfied with the job he has done and, Daniela complains, he never has any time for fun. Claudio admits that he considers fun a luxury that he cannot afford and, according to him, duty and responsibility must come first. He preaches incessantly about this to his wife, especially whenever he believes her fondness for relaxation and pleasure overcomes her needed attention to necessary duties and responsibilities.

After hearing the presentation of the couple's ambiguous request, characterized by the dilemma of duty versus pleasure, the therapist decided to activate a combined counterparadoxical intervention that would take both problems into account, that is, to pursue to the extreme both duty and pleasure. The therapist began by declaring her surprise at observing that, in spite of the couple's obvious differences, there also existed a strange convergence in the problems, at least as they had presented them: neither knew *the one thing that each of them considered most important.*

The couple were obviously confused by the therapist's statement, but their curiosity was aroused. They had always claimed they had nothing in common, yet the therapist had stated that they shared a common problem. Furthermore, neither could ignore whatever it was that each considered the most important issue. Both felt the need to ask the therapist to further explain what she meant. She replied that it was truly amazing that a man like Claudio, who was so conscious of duty and responsibility and who had always neglected everything else in his life to feel at peace with his conscience and to live up to this, had after all this time ignored *the most important of all duties.*

Claudio reflected for a while upon this; he soon realized that he did not know what the most important duty could be. At that point, the therapist stated that the most important duty was *the duty of pleasure* because only he who had already met his responsibility toward this duty was at a level to develop all other responsibilities in a healthy way. Claudio could not ignore it, therefore, if he truly wanted to fulfill every responsibility.

Daniela certainly knew this primary duty, the duty of pleasure. Nevertheless, she could not ignore *the most fundamental pleasure, the pleasure of duty*—that intense satisfaction that is experienced when she does the right things, in the right time, and in the right way.

The therapist said she recognized the values to which Daniela and Claudio had subscribed until then, and even though they were extremely diverse, it did not mean that one could be considered any better or more important than the other. Neither would she try to change these deeply rooted convictions. However, the therapist pointed out the concordant incongruence of both; neither of the two is consistent with the value that he or she professes. It is not surprising, therefore, that this would lead to a common dissatisfaction that would be more difficult to resolve if they did not respect their own values. To overcome this dilemma, she must learn the proper way to have pleasure, and he must learn the proper way to carry out his duties.

The Confused Problem The problem is presented in a confused form when it is not clear to the family which difficulties must be overcome or which problems are to be resolved. Thus, the problem is not clear to the therapist either. When the problem is defined ambiguously and when there are a number of problems, all considered of equal importance, the confusion generated creates one entire "confused problem." The therapist only knows that *a* problem exists but cannot know or identify what that problem is.

The therapist's attempts to clearly define a confused problem are, as a rule, destined to fail miserably. Instead, it is preferable to return to a confusional intervention (redefinition, prescription, or prediction), such as that used in the case of Lou and Barbara in the preceding chapter (see pp. 143–145). The confusional intervention can have therapeutic value in and of itself, or it can lead to a clearer and more articulated definition of the problem, allowing the therapy to progress in a linear way.

The Nonverbal Problem   At times the family expresses its problem or symptom mainly through analogical or non-verbal channels. With families where there is little verbal expression, the use of a nonverbal counterparadox is indicated, as in the next case:

> In the first interview, Gino was extremely con-cerned about his wife's behavior. Gloria, a woman who spoke little, recently had devel-oped strange, uncontrollable leg movements, forcing her to interrupt her professional duties as a nurse. She had undergone numerous checkups and tests, which showed no somatic illness that could justify these movements. Pre-viously attempted antianxiety therapy also proved to be unsuccessful. The leg movements appeared bizarre and unpredictable, causing much distress for her husband, who is char-acteristically methodical, precise, and very pre-dictable. He needs to be sure that everything is always under perfect control in the family. His attempts to effect this control had often been unsuccessful, even before Gloria's problem sur-faced. The three daughters in the family, like the wife, are also quiet by nature.
>
> A daily ritual in this family requires that all of them come together when he returns home from work (a clock sales business). Then he inquires of each member, in turn, what has oc-

curred during the course of the day. It upsets him that he obtains only simple, inexpressive, monosyllabic responses. Discouraged and frustrated with his inability to communicate and, therefore, to maintain control of everything, including Gloria's recent problem of uncontrollable leg movements, he is willing to try anything. He even purchased a number of books on psychology and psychiatry, thinking he might find some solution, and now, in desperation, as the situation was becoming intolerable, he consulted the therapists to determine what else was possible that he hadn't considered.

The therapists responded that if Gino really wanted to find a solution to this problem, he would have to consider something that he had evidently not tried. When he anxiously asked what they meant, he was told that he had always placed too much importance on words, while the symptoms of his wife and the behavior of his daughters indicated that it was much more important for him to pay attention to the use of *nonverbal communication*. They explained that Gino probably did not realize the full value for many people of this type of communication and, in particular, the value of the communication by the lower extremities.

The legs and the feet, as explained by the therapists, constantly transmit a tremendous amount of information by means of their position—the direction in which the feet point, the movements of the legs, and so on. Studies in experimental psychology, they continued, have shown that because words often transmit dishonest information and because facial expressions can often disguise the true message, the lower extremities are the part of the body that transmits the most honest and reliable information.

Gino was surprised to hear this; he immediately began to observe his wife's legs with much more attention than he had ever previously shown. Gloria, in response, performed a series of rapid movements with her legs. Gino then asked the therapists which books he should study in order to know more about nonverbal communication, especially regarding the legs and feet. He was given some suggestions as to what would be helpful, but they warned that nonverbal communication must essentially be studied "in the field." He was instructed to continue the daily reunions with his wife and daughters at exactly the same time, in the same way as always, and to ask the same questions, but not to expect any verbal responses. Instead, he would have to search for the answer to his questions in his family's nonverbal behaviors and, thereafter, he was to inform the therapists of the conclusions he had drawn.

In the following session, Gino seemed enthusiastic, and his wife's leg movements seemed to have diminished considerably. He gave a detailed report of the "nonverbal" meetings that had taken place; he explained that he had noticed, while observing the gestures and looks of everyone, his family's dislike for the daily interrogations. His wife, in particular, when his questions became overly insistent, began a particular movement of her feet that seemed to say she wanted to tell him to go to hell. By these movements and through other nonverbal messages, Gino could see that his wife and children considered him boring and pedantic; they seemed to want a less obsessive and more enjoyable life with him. Convinced that he had learned from this new experience, Gino asked the therapists if he could now stop the daily ritual (because, he said smiling, he didn't like being told to go to hell) and if, instead, he could take his wife out to dinner one evening. It had been many years since he had done this, and he believed it was something she would enjoy.

The therapists responded that Gino could do this if he wanted, but taking his wife out for enjoyment was not the most important thing. The important thing was whatever he would now decide to do in his relationship with his wife and children, he must always continue to make a good "field observation," never losing sight of their nonverbal responses, just as he had done this time with excellent results.

When the family returned for the next session, Gloria's legs movements had almost disappeared, and she seemed, for the first time, to be at ease and even quite talkative. Happily, she reported that her husband had taken her out to dinner, and they had a wonderful time. Then, she added, laughing, that though it

wasn't easy, Gino had even found a way to continue to follow the therapists' suggestions; he
took her to a restaurant with glass-top tables
and was, therefore, able to continue to observe
the "nonverbal messages" of her legs for the
entire evening.

The Impossible Problem   Therapists find themselves confronted with problems rather often, which, from the way
they are presented, appear to be impossible to resolve,
either from the very beginning of the therapy or at a
more advanced phase of the therapeutic process. Perhaps, at other times, the problem might not seem as
impossible, but the therapist may not be able to find an
appropriate idea for his or her intervention, or the family does not offer the cooperation necessary to the therapy. In such cases, the family's expectation for a
successful intervention does not lessen; indeed, it often
increases in proportion to the difficulty of the problem
presented.

   In such a situation the therapist may initially feel grat-
ified because he or she has received credit for having
the power to resolve an impossible problem and, if so,
can be induced to respond positively to this expectation.
He or she can, therefore, become actively engaged in
continually proposing new ideas to the family, new
points of view, and new solutions. Unfortunately, in the
majority of cases, the family does not succeed in making
good use of these ideas, but this does not reduce their
expectation that, in time, will lead the therapist into
creating new interventions which may not prove useful
to the family, and so on. Caught up in not wanting to
disappoint the family, and the need to show that he or

she is able to meet their expectations, the therapist will eventually arrive at a dead end in the forced production of new ideas. His or her resources are soon exhausted, and the family has not learned how to formulate any solutions of its own.

The counterparadoxical intervention capable of opposing the illegitimate assumption that the therapist must somehow manage to resolve everything is the one we have labelled *not having ideas*. It should be emphasized that to be successful, this type of intervention cannot be used as a simple tactic; it must correspond to a real subjective condition of the therapist. A therapist's statement that he or she has no more ideas does not have to result in losing the family, or even in getting the family to present a less impossible problem. The following case demonstrates its use:

> After many attempts to find solutions for the Arrighi family, in which the eldest son, Alessandro, was presented in therapy with a severe form of autistic withdrawal, the therapist openly acknowledged that he did not have any further ideas on how to proceed with the therapy. This statement surprised the family and they reacted with a vitality that, until then, had seemed impossible to create throughout the long course of therapy.
>
> The mother, Anita, protested to the therapist that he could not abandon them in this difficult situation. The therapist replied that he did not intend to abandon them, but he simply had to admit that, at least for the moment, he had run out of new ideas. The mother asked if he

thought he would have any in the future, and
the therapist responded that he would hope so.

With this understanding, it was agreed that
in three months the family would call again to
see if the therapist had some new ideas to propose. At the end of three months Anita called;
she was informed that, unfortunately, he still
did not have any new ideas with which to resume the interrupted treatment. Another appointment by telephone was set in another
three months; when the mother called at that
time, she said, "Yes, yes, I know you do not
have any new ideas, but I have one. May we
come for our appointment?"

The Problem Presented in an Indirect Form   As we have
seen, the family is not always in a position to clearly
define its own problem, but this does not necessarily
mean that the problem is not presented in some special
way, peculiar to a particular family. In other words,
when a family does not succeed in explicitly presenting
its difficulties, it may present them *in an indirect form.*

Implications, stories, anecdotes, and metaphor can be
other perfectly valid modalities through which to communicate the real problems. The therapist must, however, confirm the indirect modality chosen by the family
and not attempt to change it into a direct or explicit
form. In these cases, if the therapist uses a metaphor,
he or she must not choose one that would be unfamil-
iar. The therapist should, instead, use the metaphor
adopted by the family to describe the problem. Once
more, it is the family who suggests the type of interven-

tion, and the therapist must be ready to accept and to elaborate upon this suggestion in creating an *indirect counterparadoxical intervention*. For example:

> Marco is presently 42 years old, and for more than 20 years he has lived his life pent up in the house. After several different hospitalizations, without any positive results, the family decided to keep him at home, if not to cure him, at least to assist him with daily functions. Marco's behavior had been the family's main preoccupation for years: he ate only if someone fed him; he seldom spoke and then only to express disconnected thoughts; he spent all day in bed; he did not control his bowels and, most distressing of all, when from time to time he rose from the bed it was only to hit against the walls and to break anything that happened to be within reach. Often, he caused more or less serious injury to himself.
>
> In order to avoid any further consequences, the family converted his room into a genuine bunker. The glasses were unbreakable, bars were on the windows, the door was locked and, finally, all furniture and objects with which Marco could hurt himself were removed from the room.
>
> The therapy team was called for an in-home intervention, and they found themselves confronted with this homebound institutionalization that had been in operation for some time. The diagnosis of schizophrenia, which had

been confirmed many times, and the chronic, long-term nature of the problem could account for the atmosphere of resignation which existed in the family and for the absence of an actual specific request to justify the call to the team.

The mother, while describing her difficult day to the team, incidentally showed them a little blackbird that she had found in the courtyard; she kept it tied with a chain to a piece of furniture. "In the courtyard," she explained, "there are many cats and, certainly, a bird that cannot fly could not move out of range. I also cannot set the bird free in a room, because he would hit into the walls." She informed the team that she had also heard that if a bird were too long in captivity, it would acquire the scent of humans; then the other birds would avoid it and no longer accept it back into the flock. The mother turned and asked the team for their advice: should she restore the blackbird's freedom and risk it becoming easy prey for the cats in the courtyard, or should she keep it with her, at the risk of it always remaining a prisoner, never to return again to be with others of its own kind?

The indirect presentation of the problem was actually a metaphor of the situation in which both the blackbird and Marco apparently had no way out. The mother and the team were confronted with a difficult dilemma to resolve. It seemed to impose a choice between survival and independence.

The team had found in the indirect presentation of the problem the way to gain access to the psychological fortress built around Marco and his family, but the team members were not sure which would be the best way to proceed. Following a long discussion about what they could do, one member proposed asking for an opinion about what should be done with the bird at a local petshop where the elderly proprietor was well known for his vast knowledge of the living habits of birds.

Initially, the man was surprised by the question. He then said that the blackbird should be freed from the chain without exposing it to the danger of the cats immediately. It must first be taught to fly, and this should be done in one small room where there would be just enough space for the bird to use its wings. Then, later, the bird could be placed in a larger room where flying greater distances would make its wings even stronger. Only when it was observed that its wings were sufficiently strong, and it had learned to avoid obstacles, could it go out without running into serious risk. Initially the other blackbirds would shun it because they would not recognize the scent, but it would soon be accepted by them.

Marco's mother was informed of their discourse about birds without even the vaguest suggestion of any similarity to her son's situation. Nevertheless, within a few months, there proved to be a series of surprising changes.

One day, after the blackbird was in condition

to be set free, much work was initiated around the house. Marco was given a second and larger room; the mother and brother taught Marco how to move from one room to the other, and Marco learned to take long walks in this new and larger space. A few weeks later, the door was allowed to remain unlocked and even left open; Marco was allowed to walk into the hallway. Then, after seeing that his behavior was well maintained, they decided to allow him to go out of the house, even if only for a few minutes, for the first time in more than 20 years.

THE EVOLUTION OF THE PROBLEM

The presenting problem usually has a high level of stability and redundancy, *yet the problem or symptom undergoes continuous change*. Therefore, it is a matter of relative stability in the course of identifiable changes that can be of major or minor importance.

The ability to identify these changes is one of the most important gifts a therapist can possess. Whenever the therapist notices a change in the presenting problem, he or she must modify patients' suggestions, tailoring them to the new condition. Moreover, each small change can be built upon, as the starting point for the next change. If the therapist does not possess this capacity and/or work to continually exercise these skills, he or she may mistakenly persist in an attempt to obtain changes when changes have already taken place. This means that just as the problem is in continuous evolution, the therapeutic intervention must continuously be modified in order for the therapy to evolve toward ever greater change.

To construct the proper counterparadoxical intervention, a great flexibility on the part of the therapist is required, because he or she has to observe to adapt and evolve with every single case. According to this view of paradoxical therapy, as we will see in the next chapter, single cases become very important: each individual or family is able to teach the therapist a new and unique approach.

CHAPTER 10

❖❖❖❖❖❖❖❖❖❖❖❖❖❖❖❖❖❖❖❖

CLINICAL CASES

Various types of pathologies and cases of different degrees of severity require the application of different kinds of counterparadoxical interventions. This chapter offers concrete examples to demonstrate the flexibility possible in the use of therapeutic counterparadox.

THE PARADOX OF UTILIZATION

This type of therapeutic paradox represents an excellent model of confirmation of symptomatic behaviors, as the symptom is utilized to resolve itself. The self-referential character of the paradox of utilization is evident: one part of the symptom endowed with particular characteristics is utilized by the therapist to break up the totalizing structure of the same symptom.

> Carlo is the only son in a very religious family; he is extremely meticulous and methodical about everything. At 11 years of age Carlo developed an obsessive behavior which forced him and his parents to perform a series of rituals that radically altered the entire family's life. When

Carlo sat down at the table for lunch or dinner, he would begin reciting a long silent prayer that sometimes lasted for more than an hour. Carlo insisted that his parents remain silent and attentive until the prayer was finished before they could begin to eat. Prior to the onset of this symptom, Carlo's father was often late in returning home after work, never offering any explanation, but this had since changed. Now his father was forced to return home earlier. Also, because of the demands of this ritual, the mother was forced to stay at the table seated next to Carlo, whereas before she spent most of the mealtime in the kitchen. The parents had tried everything possible to stop these exhausting rituals: they pleaded, they threatened, they punished, but to no avail. Finally, they decided to bring him to a doctor who suggested family therapy.

After describing Carlo's behavior in minute detail, as well as their futile attempts to stop him, the exasperated parents asked the therapist what else they could do to resolve a problem which forced them to spend a good part of every day centered around mealtimes. The therapist told them that they must abstain from attempts to stop the prayers; instead, they must follow rigorously, and to the letter, every single direction Carlo would give them, making sure that their son carried out the prescribed tasks precisely.

They were given the following instructions: "This evening, you must obtain a stopwatch (being a very precision-oriented family, it happened that they already had one) and just at the moment you sit at the table for dinner, Mother must start the stopwatch and give Carlo the signal to begin. Carlo must then initiate a silent prayer, identical in all but one respect to his usual prayer: this prayer must be *a prayer to stop praying*. After Mother gives the signal to begin this special prayer, she must pass the stopwatch to Father who, after exactly 57 minutes, must give his son the signal to conclude the prayer to stop praying."

When the prayer required by the therapist was finished, Carlo could initiate his usual prayer and continue for as long as he wanted, and the parents must do absolutely nothing to stop him. The father would simply pass the stopwatch back to the mother in order for her to keep track of the length of time needed for the symptomatic prayer.

The prayer to stop praying must be lengthened by three minutes each time the symptomatic prayer increases in duration with respect to the preceding time.

The parents were asked to religiously monitor this process with respect to the established times. When the family returned for the next session, they reported to the therapist that since the first evening, Carlo had realized how difficult it was to carry on the stop praying prayer for the full time. He began, after only a few minutes, to beg the parents to allow him to stop, but they held firmly to the therapist's instructions and wouldn't allow him to stop before the stopwatch indicated the set time.

That first evening, the symptomatic prayer lasted exactly three minutes and the following night even less, until it had completely vanished. The parents, however, insisted that Carlo continue with the prayer to stop praying. After these first few nights, they did allow him to continue it in a shorter form after consulting with and obtaining permission from the therapist.

Within a few months the family was satisfied with the fact that the therapeutic prayer was reduced to only five minutes once a week. The parents assured the therapist that they would continue to time it precisely.

THE CONTRADICTION PARADOX

The contradiction paradox seizes upon and utilizes as a therapeutic goal the complex contradictions that exist in the symptom and in the other totalizing behaviors. The contradiction arises from the paradoxical conviction that the entire perceived reality is contained in only one single and absolute perspective.

For example, the patient who states "I am unsure about everything" is a victim of this type of contradiction, which can be exposed easily through the question, "But are you sure that you are unsure?" Both terms, "sure/unsure," though oppositional, are combined in order to demonstrate the assumption of illegitimate totality, and this can happen any time that a system of convictions or behaviors are presented as absolutes.

In practice, this type of counterparadox utilizes a term opposite to the one presented as a symptomatic behavior, and then it exposes the contradiction. It thus takes advantage of the same belief that is the basis of the assumption of illegitimate totality. The process is analogous to that followed by Godel (1931) when, in his Theorem of Incompleteness, he made use of the system of the *Principia Mathematica* in order to demonstrate the incongruence of the totalizing premises contained in the Principia itself.

In order to therapeutically effectuate the contradiction paradox, the therapist can make use of pairs of opposites—to decide/to not decide, to trust/to distrust, to control/to not control, to be dependent/to be independent and so on—making correlations between them in order to give a therapeutic sense to the contradiction that follows. The structure of this type of paradox can be the following:

- In order for you to be . . . (definition of the behavior considered to be healthy), you must be . . . (redefinition of the behavior presented as symptomatic).

or:

- In order to obtain . . . (behavior requested as healthy), you must do . . . (prescription of symptomatic behavior).

The following are examples of specific behavior correlations:

- In order to be independent, you must *first** be dependent.
- In order to *no longer* be suspicious, you must, for now, be suspicious.
- In order to obtain greater control, you must first permit yourself to lose control.
- In order to decide, you must, for now, not make any decisions.

In the following clinical case we will see how one can realize a counterparadox of contradiction in the actual therapeutic process:

> Andrea is a very attractive young woman, born into a wealthy northern Italian family. She spent her entire life trying to prove that she could get along without anyone's help—that she was independent. Refusing to listen to her parents' advice, she married and left home very young. This, she believed, would certainly show them she was independent.
>
> She married a quiet, introspective, and withdrawn man, sure that with her own open and easygoing nature she would be able to "bring him out." However, after she was married, Andrea noticed a "strange" quality in her husband's nature: not only was he extremely introverted and uncommunicative, but lately he was beginning to neglect his work. The situation was serious,

---

*As seen by these examples, therapeutic counterparadox reintroduces, through adverbs (first), or other temporal expressions (for now), the time limitations that were annulled by the undecidability of the illegitimate totality.

both psychologically and economically. Whenever Andrea tried to discuss the reasons for his stubborn silence, he would coldly reply: "I don't want to discuss it." Therefore, every attempt to confront her husband about his behavior left her feeling rejected.

In an attempt to help her husband and to try to find a way to please him, Andrea quit her job, which she thought he wanted, and gave him her full attention; she worked hard at trying to cook exquisite meals to stimulate his appetite; she made herself even more attractive to arouse him sexually; but all of her efforts proved futile and, conversely, increased his apathy. He simply continued behaving as if she didn't exist.

The young woman reported that when she went to visit her parents, she brought gifts that were very expensive, putting herself heavily in debt. She claimed she did this because her husband didn't give her enough money, and she didn't want her parents to know of the difficulties she was experiencing in her marriage.

Andrea's father had always been depressed. All her life, she believed her mother's failure at overcoming this was because she just didn't know how to get him interested and excited about life. Her mother didn't know how to have fun herself or how to cheer him up. How could she now expect him to be happy? Andrea was sure she would not repeat her mother's mistake.

In the battle to dissuade her from this early

marriage of which they disapproved, her parents had predicted failure. This made it even more difficult for the young woman to acknowledge that she was in a situation analogous to that of her mother's with her father and that neither could she succeed in changing it. She preferred to pretend that all was well with her husband, rather than admit failure to her parents.

During the interview it became clear that one thing Andrea would never relinquish was her independence. She held this as an absolute. She made it clear to the therapist that she had always done everything on her own, even if she made mistakes, and she wouldn't change this for anyone or anything.

> *Therapist:* There wouldn't be any reason to change if you were *truly* independent.
>
> *Andrea (upset):* But I am, especially with my parents, whom I have never asked for anything.
>
> *Therapist:* If you were truly independent, you would have no difficulty in speaking openly with them about your situation, but *you cannot* do this.
>
> *Andrea (insistent):* But if I tell them about my situation, it would be the same as asking for their help.
>
> *Therapist:* Not asking for their help is not proof of independence. On the contrary, it is a demonstration of the utmost

dependence: you are *dependent on your
need to prove your independence.*
Andrea: Then how can I stop this dependence
on the need to be independent?
Therapist: In order to be truly independent,
even of the need to be independent, you
must *accept* the idea that *you can* be dependent, even in facing your parents.

Andrea didn't want to be dependent, not even
on the need to be independent; for this reason,
she decided to visit her parents again, finding
the courage to tell them about her situation.
This disclosure had a surprising effect: not only
was there, for the first time, a feeling of closeness between mother and daughter through
sharing their unhappy experiences, but the
economic support that the parents could offer
allowed Andrea to no longer feel inescapably
trapped in the uncertain prospects of her husband's behavior.

As soon as it was understood that Andrea
could have both the economic means and the
"psychological independence" to go to work,
eventually needing the husband less, he quickly
abandoned his indifference in order to reclaim
Andrea's attentions and began to show re-
newed interest. "I do not know anymore if I
want to stay with my husband," confided Andrea to the therapist, "but the most important
thing is that I now know I can freely choose."

THE INCOMPLETENESS PARADOX

As we have seen in the assumption of illegitimate totality, what should be considered a simple hypothesis comes to be considered as a true and real axiom that does not need to be demonstrated. The therapeutic paradox based on the principle of incompleteness is actually established on this aspect. Without bringing into the discussion the premises and the belief systems that are at the basis of the presumed axiom, it follows its logical processes until it demonstrates its incompleteness. The demonstration of incompleteness of the presumed axiom brings about the collapse of the totalized structure without, however, challenging those aspects that demonstrate validity.

In therapeutic counterparadox the behavior or the totalized thinking of the identified patient and of the family is, therefore, confirmed. This confirmation can bring about resolution of the totality. In other words, it is not the therapist, but it is the patient's own construction that will automatically resolve his or her assumption of illegitimate totality. An example of this is offered below:

A doctor had recommended family therapy to a family with a baby affected by a serious congenital, motor, and language disorder. At the first session it became clear that the real presenting problem was not the child's handicaps. It was, instead, the stubborn conviction of the father, Paolo. He insisted that his daughter's handicaps were caused by some sort of hand pressure applied many years before by his sister (who wouldn't attend the session) to a small angioma on the baby's forehead. Paolo also insisted that the doctors who had seen his daughter were incompetent and, therefore, their diagnosis must be considered unreliable. In spite of the reassurance received regarding this, he continued to have strong doubts that his daughter's problems were caused by a congenital malformation.

While watching Paolo, the wife and the mother-in-law continued shaking their heads, making gestures to the therapist to excuse him for the absurdities he was stating. Without openly saying it, they were making every effort to get the therapist to understand that the man's ideas and his doubts were making life impossible for them.

After listening carefully to Paolo's complaints, the therapist stated emphatically that he simply did not believe that Paolo really had as much doubt as he claimed and that he had serious doubts about Paolo's doubts. Paolo looked surprised and shocked. He interrupted his recriminations about the doctor's errors and about the serious act committed by the aunt to ask the reason for the therapist's doubts about him. The therapist replied that anyone who really had such doubts, and suspected something as serious as that which he claimed, would certainly not be satisfied with such an incomplete investigation as that made by Paolo. If he really had such doubts, he would have checked much more thoroughly to verify his suspicions, and he would have sought the opinion of many other doctors. Paolo stated judiciously, "But I did consult with two different doctors, and they were both of the same opinion." The therapist replied, "Only two doctors are not enough to assure that there were no errors committed. When one has true doubts, he continually seeks even more reliable information. In this case it would first be necessary to find out which doctors would be most competent for that given problem and then, of course, to go and ask for their opinion. It wouldn't even matter how far one had to go; another city, or even to another country. You, Paolo, have done nothing of this magnitude. You didn't even worry about the fact that the doctors you have consulted are both from the same clinic and that they might have even been bribed by your sister into agreeing with her."

In spite of his firm convictions about the sister being to blame, this suspicion seemed to be too much, even to Paolo. "No, well . . . I don't believe it," Paolo stammered. "I don't think my sister could have really done such a thing." "But how can you be sure if you haven't ever checked. . . . If you haven't thoroughly investigated it?" the therapist challenged. "Actually," admitted Paolo, "I haven't seen her for some time." "Then you cannot know enough," the therapist insisted. "You have done such little investigation, that I can't take your doubts seriously, and I have to doubt them."

Gradually, Paolo began to question and criticize his own previous opinions: "Perhaps I was wrong," he stated. "In fact, my daughter was sick even before my sister touched her."

From time to time throughout the course of therapy, Paolo would again bring up this idea about his sister, but just as the therapist would suggest a thorough investigation, he would quickly ask what they could do to resolve the problems brought about because of the baby's handicaps. The therapy with the family could then proceed in this direction without being diverted.

THE REFUSAL PARADOX

In some cases the request made by the family goes against the ethics of the therapist, and if the expectation cannot be modified, the therapist can have very good reason to refuse attempting any intervention. Other reasons for which it is sometimes necessary to refuse therapy usually receive much less consideration, but they are no less important. Among these are an intense degree of overinvolvement on the part of the therapist and any sort of situation that could interfere with the therapist's freedom of choice. Loss of freedom can occur whenever the therapist feels he or she cannot work with the family's problem due to difficulties in his or her own present life circumstances, or when the presenting problem appears similar to a therapist's own unresolved personal family issues. A therapist might also consider a case too difficult, or the case may be the result of a referral which could hinder the therapeutic goal.

The therapist who makes use of confirmation to respect the family and its members' needs certainly cannot ignore his or her own needs when they surface, especially when they carry the risk of sabotaging any possible progress in the therapy. The therapist's confirmation of his or her own needs often has a remarkable therapeutic impact which corresponds effectively with a refusal of therapy: sometimes refusal can initiate a process and successful results that would not occur in a condition-free therapy situation. A refusal can be expressed in many different ways; however, there are only a few specific ways that it can be accomplished without precipitating feelings of rejection in the family and without jeopardizing the family's ability to utilize its elements as a counterparadoxical intervention. The information gathered in the initial interviews and the subsequent assessment, even if in broad outline, provides data about the most significant variables in the family system. Presumably, at the point when the therapist makes the decision to refuse therapy, he or she has been furnished with sufficient indications to give significance and therapeutic efficacy to the refusal.

> Mr. Bedini brought his wife Bianca to the therapist because she had agreed to submit to hypnosis about an event that had taken place 25 years earlier. Mr. Bedini wanted the truth. At that time Mr. Bedini returned home from work one day and found his next-door neighbor in his apartment. His wife explained that the man was a plumber and that she was having trouble

with the bathroom sink. Her husband was never satisfied with this explanation; since that day, she had never had a moment's peace. Her husband was suspicious of her every move and relentlessly questioned her about the event in order to get to the truth. For 25 years their lives were in chaos and, consequently, their children had been seriously affected as well; they often witnessed these questions and accusations, which created much emotional upset in everyone. Now this preoccupation with his suspicions was affecting his work; he received notice that he was in danger of being fired.

The therapist subsequently asked Mr. Bedini to state the reason for his request more explicitly. He said he could no longer continue to live with his suspicions. He wanted his wife to undergo hypnosis in order to be sure, once and for all, what had actually taken place 25 years ago. The following discussion ensued:

Therapist: I'm sorry, but I cannot help you.
Mr. Bedini (angrily): But you *must* do something.
Therapist: I cannot, but even if I could, I wouldn't do this for anything in the world.
Mr. Bedini (in a louder voice): But why not?
Therapist: You see, if I succeeded to clear away your doubt, and you were to discover that for 25 years you had destroyed your marriage and the lives of your wife and children for nothing, you

might suffer even greater suffering than you have until now. Therefore, please, don't ask me to help cause this. There is nothing I can do for you.

For a short time, Mr. Bedini appeared deep in thought. Then, he attempted a weak protest but was quickly discharged along with his wife. About a year later, he telephoned to ask for a new appointment:

Therapist: You know that I cannot do what you already asked me, so why have you called?

Mr. Bedini: No, it is not for that. This appointment is not for my wife. *I* need your help.

Therapist: I still do not think I can help, but I will see you with the understanding that you do not ask me again to do what I said I cannot do.

Mr. Bedini arrived for the session, with a very different affect than was evident the year before. He seemed to be somewhat less tense, and the arrogance expressed a year ago was absent.

Mr. Bedini: Unfortunately, you were right. My doubts about my wife are *almost* totally gone, but I am sick over what I have done all these years to my wife, my children, and myself. I have totally stopped tormenting them, and I decided to punish myself by working twice as hard as before. In spite of this, I continue to feel

guilty and miserable for all that I have
done to them. How can I get help?
Therapist: I cannot help you with this, even
now. I can only suggest that perhaps you
still want to maintain that little residue
of doubt that continues to remain for as
long as you can.

THE PATIENT-THERAPIST PARADOX

In this type of therapeutic intervention the therapist
does not limit himself or herself to confirming the identified patient's symptomatic behavior; instead he or she
accepts it to the point of acting as if it were his or her
own. In this way, the therapist takes the symptom from
the patient, who is then free to develop alternative behaviors. It is a form of counterparadoxical intervention
based on the relationship that the family system and its
members have with the therapist. To be used most effectively, this type of paradox requires an already well-
established therapeutic relationship; therefore, its use
in the early stages of therapy would be a mistake.

It must be particularly emphasized that this intervention cannot be used simply for the purpose of expe-
diency; it must correspond to an actual way of thinking
and feeling, which the therapist can utilize in a therapeutic sense. It is only in this type of situation that both
the patient and the family will be able to develop em-
pathy toward the therapist, which will become the key
to access change. The therapist in using this type of
counterparadoxical modality must be willing to exchange roles at least temporarily and, then, to accept

the help that the family and the identified patient will offer.

Carmine and his wife Adele came to therapy for about a year because of his depression. Habitually, Carmine began every session with a long series of complaints. He monotonously bemoaned the fact that he couldn't manage to get ahead, that he was unable to get any satisfaction out of life, and that he wasn't getting any benefit out of therapy. Inevitably, Adele would soon join this ritual, complaining about all the things that her husband's depression kept her from doing: she couldn't have friendships because he didn't like having people around; she couldn't go out because she couldn't leave him alone, and she often had to neglect taking care of herself and the house, as he constantly kept her occupied taking care of him.

In this last session, the usual script was repeated with customary regularity for at least 20 minutes until the therapist, now exasperated, interrupted the laments of the couple:

Therapist: I want to tell you truthfully about how I felt about how you felt when you arrived for your session today. I felt deeply discouraged at the thought that everything would be as always. Unfortunately, it has gone exactly as I thought, and just as I feared; nothing has changed from the last session until today. I realized it looking at your faces as

soon as you came in; but now that it has
been confirmed by your words, it is even
more difficult to bear the misery of my
failure. It saddens and discourages me
to the point where I doubt that I can be
of any help to you today.

I'm not even sure if I can be of any
help in the future, because I have the
impression that every time I see you, I'll
be forced to find myself faced with the
proof that this therapy has been a failure, and I don't know if I can continue
to tolerate this unpleasant state of mind.

Adele: You mustn't be so depressed; there is
no reason for you to take it all on. Things
did not go as bad as they might seem.

Carmine: Since we have started coming here,
our relationship is much better; indeed
...perhaps we should let you know
that. . . .

Adele: Yes, we must tell you this. We have
decided. . .after much uncertainty about
ourselves and our marriage. . . well, we
have finally decided that we want to have
a baby.

The therapist began to ask himself why it was
that these positive evaluations, and the decision
to have a baby which they were so happy to
report, had not been communicated to him by
the couple, before, in the first part of the session.

Therapist: What you have said does not make me feel any better. I deceived myself other times when I noted an improvement, and every time I was wrong. I can no longer allow myself to believe there is any real improvement. I have already had enough disappointment.

Carmine: You are too pessimistic. I want to assure you that the improvement is real, and it will last for a long time.

Therapist: I appreciate your attempts to make me feel better, but unfortunately today I cannot see anything other than an irreparable situation, for which I alone am responsible.

Carmine: I cannot continue to listen to you talk like this, and to see you so depressed.

Adele: Maybe we can do something for you?

Therapist: Unfortunately I don't believe anything can be done.

Carmine: Perhaps with hypnosis. I remember when you did this to us, I felt much better. I can find out how to do this to you, or something like it, if you will allow me.

Therapist: The problem is that this is your session, not mine. You came here to improve your situation, not mine. Therefore, even if you managed to make me feel better, I'm sorry to say that you would still have to pay for the hour. . . .

Adele: Look, if you would no longer feel this demoralized and depressed, it would

benefit us, too. So don't worry about the
payment. This is still our therapy, and
we want to continue it with the therapist
in good shape.

Carmine knows how to do hypnosis.
He learned it from a friend; he regularly
uses it on himself at home, when he has
one of his usual headaches and cannot
sleep. It almost always makes him feel
better; therefore, I think you can trust
him.

Carmine (after a few minutes): Now, doctor,
close your eyes and relax, you must only
think about pleasant things; everything
is well and good, and you can be content.
All your worries will disappear and will
leave in their place deep serenity: you
can dream or imagine anything that you
like . . . only things that bring pleasure,
nothing sad or worrisome. . . .

The hypnosis proceeded and then Carmine directed the therapist to again awaken:

Therapist: I must acknowledge that it went
very well. I succeeded in not thinking of
unpleasant things and I had two very
pleasant dreams instead. The first
dream is very personal, and therefore I
think I will not talk about it; but in the
second dream, I saw both of you together with a newborn baby. Of course,
it was only a dream, but I must tell you

that you looked like you were very happy
and smiling.

You mustn't consider my telling you
this as encouragement to have the baby
that you now want. Therefore, I do not
believe that the dream holds any value
for you, but it certainly had value for me
in that I could forget for a short time all
the disappointment and see you happy,
at least in the dream.

For the first time, after a full year of therapy,
the following session did not begin with the
usual complaints. Indeed, Carmine and Adele
finally appeared for therapy smiling and looking prudently satisfied with their situation, but
from that time on they continued to very carefully observe every little reaction by the therapist.

CONTRAINDICATIONS OF
PARADOXICAL THERAPY

Dangerous or Harmful Behaviors

When understood as a general principle, therapeutic
counterparadox along with a therapist's attitude prove
its validity despite the various contingencies that may
occur in the course of the therapeutic process. However,
translating this attitude into techniques for intervention
necessarily requires an accurate assessment of both indications and contraindications of the therapeutic

counterparadox. The use of counterparadox is not justified as a prescription or positive redefinition when confronting behaviors which are considered *dangerous or harmful* to oneself or to others. Both for ethical and legal reasons, to say nothing of the actual risks that situations of this type can pose, we advise against the use of paradox in cases where behaviors are determined to be suicidal or aggressive or in cases of drug addiction, anorexia, and other dangerous disorders. Suggestions that one shoot up drugs, drink to oblivion, not eat, or attempt suicide can never be part of a therapeutic intervention, even if cases are reported in the literature that indicate the opposite.

Suggestions of this type have been given with the belief that counterparadox will somehow obtain a reverse effect, but there is no way to guarantee this outcome. When one prescribes a behavior, there is always the possibility that that behavior will actually be carried out. When using a paradoxical intervention one must consider in advance the possibility of both eventualities:

1. That the prescription will not be carried out.
2. That the prescription will be carried out.

In a counterparadoxical intervention, it is the freedom to choose between the two alternatives that allows the identified patient and his family to resolve the undecidability in which they are caught. The therapist must, therefore, be ready to accept both of the possible choices, and he or she cannot accept both when dangerous behaviors are prescribed. However, in these cases, one can use other modalities of counterparadoxical intervention, such as *"splitting"* or the *use of fantasy*.

SPLITTING (LANKTON & LANKTON, 1986)

This consists of a prescription that is put into effect after having divided the symptom or the behavior considered as dangerous into a series of successive steps. In practice, the therapist looks for the behaviors that precede the actions that he wants to eliminate and prescribes one of these behaviors to the point of improving control. In this way the patient can stop before arriving at the final undesired behavior. One can, for example, prescribe the control of sensations of discomfort that precede anger that might otherwise transform into violent behavior later.

THE USE OF ALTERNATIVE FANTASIES (WHITAKER, 1977)

This consists of suggesting different fantasies about the harmful behaviors that run the risk of taking place. For example, to a woman who had attempted suicide, the therapist said, "If you wanted to murder your husband, how would you do it?" Whitaker also suggests acting on the same symptom through separating interpersonal stress and intrapersonal fantasy stress, that is, to expand, by means of fantasy, the possible and often undesired implications. For example, a patient who had expressed suicidal ideation was asked to think about how long her husband's sadness would last if she were deceased; who her husband would marry after her death; how long the sadness of the children would last; and if, after her death, her husband would entrust the children's care to her mother-in-law. In this way, the intrapersonal stress is redirected to an interpersonal level; moreover, this is the type of intervention in which fantasies are made accessible through open discussion between the family members, which allows the family to improve their communication repertory.

Rules of the Therapeutic Setting

One contraindication for the application of counterparadox is represented by the rules of the therapeutic setting that concern the administrative organization of the therapeutic context. A paradoxical prescription cannot be applied to these rules, as they correspond to the limits to which the therapist can extend the confirmation of the dysfunctional behaviors.

The therapist cannot delegate to the family the disposition of his "operating room" and the use of his "instruments." This is the area in which the therapist can establish with greatest efficacy what Bowen (1972) defined as the "I position," and it is in this area that the family will usually attempt to test the therapist's strength. (In all other areas it is up to the family to define its "I position.") A therapist who is not able to clearly establish these "I position" norms, or cannot make them respected, will experience great difficulty in trying to lead the therapy toward a desired outcome.

The rules of the therapeutic setting are prerequisites for therapy, but in a certain sense they are also a part of the therapy inasmuch as the attitude of the therapist toward them informs the family on how to behave with their own rules. They also represent an indirect, but very effective, way to bring about change in the family organization.

When the family violates these rules, or demonstrates

little interest in following them, the therapist certainly cannot resolve the problem with a counterparadoxical intervention. Aside from those disadvantages that could arise for the therapist, it would in fact be useless on the outcome level, and also a little ridiculous to positively redefine the session's unpaid fee or to prescribe that a family continue to be late for the sessions. It is, instead, much more advantageous to have a prior agreement with the family about the rules that they will uphold and, therefore, to ask that they respect them. Otherwise, in the more serious cases, therapy could be interrupted or declared futile.

THE THERAPIST

In current literature, therapeutic paradox is often described as some type of secret weapon that must be used against an adversary who is particularly difficult to handle. However, the family—although they present with problems and inadequacies—is not to be made into an enemy, and the therapy cannot be considered a war.

In our opinion, to be used with coherence and efficacy, the therapeutic paradox must not be considered a weapon, an instrument of control, or a trick. We consider counterparadox a specific tool for the resolution of an illegitimate totality. The function of this tool is to restore, for victims of the undecidability, the freedom to make choices which had previously been lost.

Therapeutic paradox, at least as we intend its use, is based essentially on a general attitude of confirmation toward symptomatic behaviors. Therefore, in order to use it coherently with this view, the therapist must find in the behaviors some aspects that he or she regards as valid, to the point where they can be confirmed honestly.

In order to succeed in this endeavor, the therapist must not be content with only his or her first observations. The aspects of the symptom that can be considered valid and can be confirmed by the therapist are usually slightly evident or even completely hidden. Often, they are not culturally accepted and are recognizable only when the entire system is carefully evaluated in all its complexity, taking into account the diverse levels of which it consists.

The road toward correct usage of counterparadox cannot be reached by instinct, and to begin is not easy. Much preparation is required for one to discover the less obvious side of human interactions. It is a continuous exercise to enter and exit from the closely observed system in order to perform proper observations from a series of different perspectives. The therapist who uses paradox is, therefore, obliged to effect changes in himself analogous to those which he expects to achieve with the family. In this sense, counterparadox is a sort of crucible of the therapist's good faith—a demonstration of the ability to believe in what one says and in what one does. When the therapist does not succeed in finding counterparadox endowed with this authenticity, when he or she does not truly believe in its premises, then it is preferable that the therapist restrains from using it.

LOGICAL TERMS
GLOSSARY

Ambiguity: the property of a given proposition to assume many possible values or meanings. Ambiguity can be *simple* when it involves only one logical type, and *systematic* when the ambiguous term belongs simultaneously to different logical types.

Class: constituted by all the terms that have the relationship "x" with other terms. It can also be said that all the objects satisfying a propositional function form a class. In other words, every propositional function determines a class, so that two functions that are formally equivalent determine the same class while, conversely, two functions that determine the same class are formally equivalent.

Fallacy: a paradox or any other logical construction in which a mistake in reasoning has been discovered.

Illegitimate totality: arises when one member of the collection contains the same collection. Its prerequisite is the systematic ambiguity.

Logical type: the range of significance of some function. The first (or lowest) type is composed of terms or individuals; the second is composed of classes; the third is composed of classes of classes.

Metalanguage: a language that is used by scientists in order to describe, discuss, and calculate a certain discipline. For example, mathematics can be used to discuss logic or the same mathematics (metamathematics). Human beings can use communication to comment on their way of communicating (metacommunication) or sophisticated languages for describing their behavior and interaction patterns.

Propositional function: a function that contains a variable *x* and that expresses a proposition as soon as a value is assigned to *x*. The propositional function differs from a common mathematical function; its values are propositions and form a common proposition because of its inherent ambiguity. The ambiguity of a propositional function depends on its undetermined variable.

Range of significance: the range of values among which the variable should be contained in order for the propositional function to have meaning.

Symbolic (or formal) logic: a logic that is based on the use of mathematical symbols.

Term or individual: any object that is not a range of values.

Undecidability: a consequence of the vicious circle that brings a paradox; an endless oscillation of meanings makes it impossible to decide if a certain proposition or communication is true or false.

Variable: in *mathematics*, an undetermined number or quantity; in *symbolic logic*, any symbol whose meaning is not determined.

Vicious circle: an infinite recurring of the same pattern in reasoning (or in human interaction) that does not allow one to recognize a definite meaning (or to have access to learning) and creates a paradox. It is the consequence of a violation of the logical types by an assumption of illegitimate totality.

BIBLIOGRAPHY

Andolfi, M. (1977). *La terapia con la famiglia [Therapy with the family]*. Roma, Italy: Astrolabio.

Aristotle (1946). Book V. In W.D. Ross (Ed.), *The works of Aristotle* (12 volumes). Oxford, England: Oxford University Press. (The 12 volumes were published between 1908–1952)

Aristotle (1966). *Metaphysics*. Ann Arbor, MI: Ann Arbor Paperbacks, University of Michigan Press.

Ashby, W. R. (1956). *An introduction to cybernetics*. London, England: Chapman. (Italian translation: Ashby, W. R. [1971] *Introduzione alla cibernetica*, Torino, Italy: Einaudi.)

Bateson, G. (1942). Social planning and their concept of deutero-learning. In L. Bryson & L. Finkelstein (Eds.), *Science, philosophy and religion* (New York, Conference on Science, Philosophy and Religion in Their Relation to the Democratic Way of Life, Inc., pp. 81–97).

Bateson, G., & Ruesh, J. (1951). *Communication: The social matrix of psychiatry*. New York: Norton.

Bateson, G. (1953). The position of humor in human communication. In H. Von Foerster (Ed.), *Transactions of the ninth conference on cybernetics, 1952 (pp. 1–47)*. New York: Macy Foundation.

Bateson, G. (1955). A theory of play and fantasy; a report on theoretical aspects of the project for study of the role of paradoxes of abstraction in communication. In *Approaches to the study of human personality, Psychiatric Research Reports*, No. 2 (pp. 39–51). Washington, DC: American Psychiatric Association.

Bateson, G., Jackson, D. D., Haley, J., & Weakland, J. H. (1956). Toward a theory of schizophrenia. *Behavioral Science* (1)*4*, 251–264.

Bateson, G. (1960a). The group dynamic of schizophrenia. In L. Appleby, J.M. Scher, J. Cummings (Eds.), *Chronic schizophrenia:*

Explorations in theory and treatment (pp. 90–105). Glencoe, IL: The Free Press.

Bateson, G. (1960b). Minimal requirements for a theory of schizophrenia. *Archives of General Psychiatry* (1)2, 154–161.

Bateson, G., Jackson, D. D., Haley, J., & Weakland, J.H. (1963). A note on double bind. *Family Process, 2,* 477–491.

Bateson, G. (1966). Problems in cetacean and other mammalian communication. In K.S. Norris (Ed.), *Whales, dolphins and porpoises.* Berkeley and Los Angeles, CA: University of California Press.

Bateson, G. (1968). Redundancy and coding. In T.A. Sebeok (Ed.), *Animal communication: Technique of study and results of research.* Bloomington, IN: Indiana University Press.

Bateson, G., (1971a). The cybernetic self: A theory of alcoholism. *Psychiatry, 34,* 1–18.

Bateson, G. (1971b). Style, grace and information in primitive art. In A. Forge (Ed.), *The study of primitive art.* Oxford, England: Oxford University Press.

Bateson, G. (1972a). *Steps to an ecology of the mind.* New York: Ballantine.

Bateson, G. (1972b). The logical categories of learning and communication, and the acquisition of world views. In G. Bateson, *Steps to an ecology of the mind.* New York: Ballantine.

Bateson, G. (1976). Double bind 1969. In C. E. Sluzki & D. C. Ransom (Eds.), *Double bind: The foundation of the communicational approach to the family.* New York: Grune & Stratton.

Bateson, G. (1978). The birth of a matrix or double bind and epistemology. In M. Berger (Ed.), *Beyond the double bind.* New York: Brunner/Mazel.

Bateson, G. (1979). *Mind and nature.* London, England: Wildwood House.

Bochenski, J.M. (1970). *A history of formal logic.* New York: Chelsea Publishers.

Boole, G. (1847). *The mathematical analysis of logic.* London, England: Cambridge.

Bowen, M. (1972). Toward a differentiation of a self in one's family. In J. L. Framo (Ed.), *Family interaction.* New York: Springer.

Canevelli, F., Loriedo, C., Pezzi, D., Trasarti Sponti, W., & Vella, G. (1981). La prescrizione [Prescriptions]. In G. Vella (Ed.) *Psicoterapia relazionale [Relational psychotherapy].* Roma, Italy: Bulzoni.

Cronen, V. E., Johnson, K.M., & Lannaman, J. W. (1982). Paradoxes, double binds, and reflexive loops: An alternative theoretical perspective. *Family Process, 21* (1), 91–112.

Dell, P. (1982). Beyond homeostasis: Toward a concept of coherence. *Family Process, 21*(1), 21–41.

Dell, P. (1986). Why do we continue to call them paradoxes? *Family Process, 25*(2), 223–234.

de Shazer, S. (1980). Brief family therapy: A metaphorical task. *Journal of Marital and Family Therapy, 6*(4), 471–476.

Diogenes, L. (1950–1951). *Lifes of eminent philosophers* (2 volumes) (R. D. Hicks, Trans.). London, England: Cambridge.

Engels, F. (1984). *Anti-Duhring: Herr Eugen Duhring's revolution in science.* Chicago: C. H. Kerr.

Ekman, P. (1985). *Telling lies: Clues to deceit in the marketplace, politics and marriage.* New York: Norton.

Erickson, M. H. (1958). Naturalistic techniques of hypnosis. *American Journal of Clinical Hypnosis, 1*, 3–8.

Erickson, M. H. (1964a). An hypnotic technique for resistant patients; the patient, the technique and its rationale and field experiments. *American Journal of Clinical Hypnosis, 7*, 8–32.

Erickson, M. H. (1964b). The confusion technique in hypnosis. *American Journal of Clinical Hypnosis, 6*, 183–207.

Erickson, M. H. (1965). The use of symptoms as an integral part of hypnotherapy. *American Journal of Clinical Hypnosis, 8*, 41–57.

Erickson, M. H., Rossi, E. L., & Rossi, S. I. (1976). *Hypnotic realities: The induction of clinical hypnosis and forms of indirect suggestion.* New York: Irvington.

Erickson, M. H. (1980). In E. L. Rossi (Ed.), *Collected papers of Milton H. Erickson* (Vol. IV). New York: Irvington.

Farrelly, F., & Brandsma, J. M. (1974). *Provocative therapy.* Fort Collins, CO: Shield Publishing.

Fisch, R., Weakland, J. H., & Segal, L. (1982). *The tactics of change: Doing therapy briefly.* San Francisco, CA: Jossey Bass.

Frankl, V. E. (1939). Aur medikamentaosen unterstutzung der psychotherapie bei neurosen [A medical understanding of the psychotherapy of the neuroses]. *Schweizer Archiv fur Neurologie und Psychiatrie, 43*, 26–31.

Frankl, V. E. (1947). *Die psychotherapie in der praxis.* [*Psychotherapy in practice*] Vienna, Austria: Deuticke.

Frege, G. (1879). *Begriffsshcrift, eine der Arithmetisken Nachgebildete Formelsprache des reinen Denkens.* Halle, Germany: Pohle.

Frege, G. (1893–1903). *Grundgesetze der Arithmetik.* Jena, Germany: Pohle.

Godel, K. (1931). Ubel formal unentscheidhbare satze der Principia Mathematica und verwandter systeme I [On formally undecidable propositions of principia mathematica and related systems I]. *Monatsh. Math. Phys., 38*, 173–198.

Grunebaum, H., & Chasin, R. (1978). Relabeling and reframing reconsidered: The beneficial effects of a pathological label. *Family Process, 17*, 449–456.

Halbwachs, F. (1984). Causalita' lineare e causalita' circolare in fisica [Linear and circular causality in physics]. In M. Bunge (Ed.), *Le teorie della causalita'* [*Theories of causality*]. Torino, Italy: Einaudi.

Haley, J. (1963). *Strategies of psychotherapy.* New York: Grune & Stratton.

Haley, J. (1973). *Uncommon therapy: The psychiatric techniques of Milton H. Erickson.* New York: Norton.

Haley, J. (1976). *Problem solving therapy.* San Francisco, CA: Jossey-Bass.

Haley, J. (1984). *Ordeal therapy: Unusual ways to change behavior.* San Francisco, CA: Jossey-Bass.

Haley, J. (1986). *Uncommon therapy: The psychiatric techniques of Milton H. Erickson* (2nd ed.). New York: Norton.

Henry, J. (1973). *Pathways to madness.* New York: Vintage Books.

Hilbert, D. (1928). Die grundlagen der mathematic. *Abhandlunghen ans dem mathematischen Seminar der Hamburgischen Universitat, 6*, 65–85.

Hofstadter, D. (1979). *Godel, Escher, Bach: An eternal golden braid.* New York: Basic Books.

Howard, N. (1971). *Paradoxes of rationality: Theory of metagames and political behavior.* Cambridge, MA: MIT Press.

Hughes, P., & Brecht, G. (1979). *Vicious circles and infinity: An anthology of paradox.* New York: Penguin Books.

Jantsch, E. (1980). *The self-organizing universe.* Oxford, England: Pergamon.

Keeney, B. P. (1983). *Aesthetics of change.* New York: Guilford.

Kierkegaard, S. A. (1944). *Aut-aut.* Milano, Italy: Denti.

Kirk, G. (1962). *The presocratic philosophers.* New York: Cambridge University Press.

Lankton, S., & Lankton, C. (1986). *Enchantment and intervention in family therapy.* New York: Brunner/Mazel.

Le Moigne, J. P. (1985). Progettazione della complessita' e complessita' della progettazione [The design of complexity and the complexity of design]. In G. Bocci & M. Ceruti (Eds.), *La sfida della complessita'* [*The challenge of complexity*]. Milano, Italy: Feltrinelli.

Levick, S. E. (1983). Paradox of always-never land. In Wolberg & Aronson, *Group and family therapy.* New York: Brunner/Mazel.

Madanes, C. (1980). Protection, paradox, and pretending. *Family Process, 19*(1), 73–86.

Madanes, C. (1984). *Behind the one-way mirror.* San Francisco, CA: Jossey-Bass.

Mehrabian, A. (1981). *Silent messages: Implicit communication of emotions and attitudes.* Delmont, CA: Wadsworth.

Minuchin, S. (1974). *Families and family therapy.* Cambridge, MA: Harvard University Press.

Montaigne, M. (1959). *Complete Essays.* Massachussetts: Stanford College, University Press.

Morin, E. (1977). *La Methode I, La Nature de la Nature* [*Methods I, The nature of nature*]. Paris, France: Editions du Seuil.

Morin, E. (1980). *La Methode II, La Vie de la Vie* [*Methods II, The life of life*]. Paris, France: Editions du Seuil.

Nagel, E. & Newman, J. R. (1958). *Godel's proof.* New York: New York University Press.

Newton, J. R. (1968). Considerations for the psychotherapeutic technique of symptom rescheduling. *Psychotherapy: Theory, Research and Practice, 5,* 95–103.

Quine, W. V. (1962). Paradox. *Scientific American,* 206.

Quine, W. V. (1966). *The ways of paradox and other essays.* New York: Random House.

Racamier, P. (1983). *Gli schizofrenici* [Schizophrenics]. Milano, Italy: Cortina.

Rohrbaugh, M., Tennen, H., Press, S., & White, L. (1981). Compliance, defiance and therapeutic paradox. *American Journal of Orthopsychiatry, 51,* 454–467.

Rose, V. (1886). Librorum Fragmenta. In *Aristotelis Opera,* Leipzig, Ed. Acad. reg. bor.

Russell, B. (1903). *The principles of mathematics.* London: Cambridge University Press.

Russell, B. (1908). Mathematical logic as based on the theory of types. *American Journal Mathematics, 30,* 222–262.

Russell, B. (1919). *Introduction to mathematical philosophy.* London, England: Cambridge.

Seltzer, L. F. (1986). *Paradoxical strategies in psychotherapy: A comprehensive overview and guidebook.* New York: Wiley.

Selvini Palazzoli, M., Boscolo, L., Cecchin, G., & Prata, G. (1978). *Paradox and counterparadox.* New York: Jason Aronson.

Sluzki, C. E., & Ransom, D. C. (1976). *Double bind: The foundation of the communicational approach to the family.* New York: Grune & Stratton.

Sluzki, C. E. (1987). L'effimera natura del paradosso in terapia [The ephemeral nature of paradox in therapy]. *Attraverso lo Specchio, 15–17*, 23–27.

Smullyan, R. M. (1978). *What is the name of this book?* London: Prentice Hall.

Stanton, M. D. (1981). Strategic approach to family therapy. In A.S. Gurman & D. D. Kniskern (Eds.), *Handbook of family therapy.* New York: Brunner/Mazel.

Von Bertalanffy, L. (1968). *General systems theory.* New York: Braziller.

Watzlawick, P. (1965). Paradoxical predictions. *Psychiatry, 28,* 368–374.

Watzlawick, P., Beavin, J. E., & Jackson, D. D. (1967). *Pragmatics of human communication.* New York: Norton.

Watzlawick, P., Weakland, J., & Fisch, R. (1974). *Change: Principles of problem formation and problem resolution.* New York: Norton.

Watzlawick, P. (1981). Riddles of self reflexiveness. In C. Wilder & J. H. Weakland (Eds.), *Rigor and imagination: Essays from the legacy of Gregory Bateson.* New York: Praeger.

Weakland, J. H., Fisch, R., Watzlawick, P., & Bodin, A. M. (1974). Brief therapy: Focused problem resolution. *Family Process, 13,* 141–168.

Weeks, G. R. (Ed.). (1991). *Promoting change through paradoxical therapy, revised edition.* New York: Brunner/Mazel.

Weeks, G. R., & L'Abate, L. (1982). *Paradoxical psychotherapy: Theory and practice with individuals, couples and families.* New York: Brunner/Mazel.

Whitaker, C. A. (1977). The importance to the family therapist of being impotent. *The Family, 4,2,* 67–74.

Whitehead, A. N., & Russell, B. (1910). *Principia mathematica.* London: Cambridge University Press.

Whorf, B. L. (1956). *Language, thought and reality.* Cambridge, MA: Technical Press of MIT.

Wilden, A. & Wilson, T. (1976). The double bind: Logic, magic, and economic. In C. E. Sluzki & D. C. Ransom (Eds.), *Double bind: The foundation of the communicational approach to the family.* New York: Grune & Stratton.

Wittgenstein, L. (1980). *Tractatus logico-philosophicus.* Torino, Italy: Einaudi.

Zeig, J. K. (1980). Symptom prescription techniques: Clinical applications using elements of communication. *American Journal of Clinical Hypnosis, 23,* 23–33.

NAME INDEX

SUBJECT INDEX

ABOUT THE AUTHORS

CAMILLO LORIEDO, M.D., is a Psychiatrist with the Psychiatric Clinic, University of Rome, School of Medicine; and he is the Director, Center for Couple and Family Psychotherapy of Rome. Dr. Loriedo is author of *Terapia relazionale: le tecniche e i terapeuti* and is editor of several other books on family therapy and Ericksonian hypnosis.

GASPARE VELLA, M.D., is Professor of Psychiatry and Director of the Psychiatric Clinic, University of Rome; and Director, School of Psychiatry, University of Rome. He is author of over 200 scientific articles and books on clinical psychiatry and he has studied and practiced family and couples therapy for more than 20 years.